Never forget:
Every step counts!
To your success,
Shannon

THE 5°
PRINCIPLE

How Small Changes
Lead to Big Results

SHANNON CASSIDY
Executive Coach / Speaker / Facilitator

Potential Publishing
Philadelphia, PA
www.5degreeprinciple.com

ISBN: 978-0-9886122-0-4

Printed in the USA.

DEDICATION

Ryan and Grace, it is a privilege to be your Mom.

Mike, it is a blessing to be your wife.

CONTENTS

FOREWORD

Sharon Lechter
Founder and CEO of Pay Your Family First
Spokesperson for National CPAs Financial Literacy Commission
Co-author of *Outwitting the Devil*, *Three Feet From Gold*
and *Rich Dad Poor Dad*

Each and every one of us is where we are in our lives today because of the decisions and choices we have made along the way. I am reminded of the expression, "Today is the first day of the rest of your life." Realizing if we want something different out of life, we need to start making different choices.

In *The Five Degree Principle*, Shannon Cassidy provides you with a blueprint to support your learning to "choose" a better life. It serves as a practical guide on how you can change your attitudes and perspectives, to quickly move you closer to your goals, one small step at a time. Moreover, Shannon does an outstanding job in reducing complexities to simple, practical techniques that will liberate you from indecision and empower you to take control of your destiny. You'll feel your self-confidence skyrocket along the way.

The book's main character, Lauren, rides a very realistic (and often very familiar) roller coaster of highs and lows in both her personal and professional life. At first, accepting her employer's offer to work with an executive coach was both threatening and intimidating. Though skeptical, Lauren starts seeing improvements, learns how to refocus her lens on life and makes shifts to move from a victim/blame mindset to a victor mindset. The coach's invaluable insights help her turn the corner. The story exemplifies a shift from inaction due to fear…to acting in spite of fear…and overcoming self-limiting beliefs.

I encourage you to take a step. Try some of Shannon's five degree principles in your own life. You're closer to what you're aiming for than you think.

ACKNOWLEDGMENTS

This book has been a team effort. My coaches, clients, friends, family and editors have all helped to contribute to the ideas offered here. The team of coaches and supporters who offered tremendous help: Mom, Cathryn, Shyanne, Steve, Cathy, Rick, Ginny, and many others. *Thank you!*

Thanks to the **bridge between, inc.** Board of Advisors: Mike, Cathryn, Rob, Carrie, Loren, Megan, Tom, Eileen, Tony, Katie, Vince, and Stephanie. I'm grateful for your generous advice, counsel, encouragement and support.

I thank my lifetime mentor, coach, and dear friend Dr. Agnes Doody. You taught me how to write, express myself, face challenges, take chances, and live life to the fullest. Your purple correction pen, fun letters, and treasured friendship enrich my life beyond measure.

My late Grandpa John Broda, descendant of Polish immigrant parents, lent me the funding to start bridge between, inc. in 2000. He had so much joy helping me become an American business owner, fulfilling my vision of helping people. He lives on in my appreciation for our business and the dedicated work ethic he passed down.

I want to acknowledge the support and love of my parents, Ray and Maureen Buckley and my sister Kelly McMahon. Your generous love and faith nurture me as an invaluable source of strength. I love you.

My dog Jake. He has been my loyal companion since he joined our family. Life lessons I learn from him: take it easy, be consistent, have patience, forgive easily and get excited to see people you love.

My children Ryan and Grace – your curiosity, spirit and joie de vivre provide a fresh perspective to life's complexity and beauty. You've taught me a new depth to my abilities to love, to exhibit patience and to play. Sadly, I still haven't mastered the hula hoop. Thank you for the joy of sharing life together. You make me so happy. You are enough.

Most of all, my deepest strength and encouragement comes from my husband Mike. You are my rock. You're a true gentleman. Your character, patience and genuine goodness are such a positive influence. Thank you for being my life partner, my teacher and my best friend.

My life mission is to serve God by choosing love. Face fear and do it anyway — *with love*. The choice we make each day is to live in fear (anxiety, frustration, anger, disappointment) or love (joy, compassion, generosity, freedom). I choose love. My mission for this book is to contribute something to help guide and strengthen others, whatever they undertake. I'm thankful for the opportunity to share what has been put in my heart. May it be pleasing.

INTRODUCTION

Wish you could pay off your debt? Lose weight? Earn more? Get promoted? Have more "balance"? Too much work, you may think. Why bother? Through no apparent fault of our own, from time to time many of us feel stuck. As if we're marching in place, have lost our momentum, not going anywhere. That feeling can apply to our personal relationships, our golf or tennis games too. But most often it surfaces in our careers.

The trick is: baby steps. Small shifts. Five degree shifts, rather than one-hundred-eighty degree turns. Attempting to effect huge changes can be overwhelming and hinder efficiently reaching one's objectives. Making change five degrees at a time is a more successful means to reaching objectives. Those small five degree shifts add up significantly in our quest to reach a more desired destination.

Small changes lead to big results.

As a professional coach with executives and sales teams at Fortune 100 companies, including Comcast and Time Warner and many others, I've encountered so many talented, technically competent professionals who believe they should be further along in their careers than they are. They often think one of two things:

The cards are — the system is — somehow stacked against them. If only they'd attended the "right" school, met the "right" people, partnered happily, been born wealthy, or played the game of life and business smarter, advances, promotions, fortune and fame would be within their grasp.

It will take huge risks, amazing luck, or monumental changes to make their lives better. Miracles, almost. Like Moses, they want to be able to part the Red Sea, but when that doesn't happen, they give up. My situation *is what it is*, they convince themselves.

I believe — and my experience tells me — that these stories and assumptions are simply not true. They are myths.

First, there is no stack of cards that determines where an individual is right now or where they're going. There are only stacks of choices. Stacks of attitudes. Stacks of desires.

Second, monumental, miraculous changes rarely occur in real life. Real changes happen gradually or in small increments. Bite sizes. Tweaks. Polishing and fine-tuning.

> **Real changes happen gradually or in small increments.**

This book will demonstrate the path to progress. Not in leaps and bounds, but in small, deliberate, intentional changes — five degrees at a time. Life, and thus change, is a journey. And despite the inevitable challenges, that journey can and should be an enjoyable one.

I invite you to join fictional friend Lauren Colton on her journey as she finds meaning and purpose in her career, parenting, and life. Lauren will face demanding situations throughout this story. She has her disappointments and setbacks, confronting the "ol' boy" network, feeling she's been singled out for career stagnation by an unfeeling, heartless organization. But, with the help of a strategic professional leadership coach, her hard work and creativity pay off. The small shifts she makes in pursuit of her goals ultimately lead to major changes in her outcomes. Lauren proves to herself that she is unstoppable.

Champions always find a way to succeed! Even if the score says they've lost, individuals and teams who play full out and learn from setbacks truly win.

—Shannon Cassidy

Demonstrate Resilience

"In order to succeed, people need a sense of self-efficacy, to struggle together with resilience to meet the inevitable obstacles and inequities of life."

—Albert Bandura

Psychologist and Teacher

We're stronger than we think. Setbacks and challenges are part of life. Effectively learning from setbacks and rebounding from challenges is what differentiates suffering from success.

Lauren is confronted with bad news. She must be the model of resilience – the human ability to recover from disappointment – in order to save face – and her career.

◆ ◆ ◆

Lauren Colton believed her career was the one remaining area of her life over which she could exert some control. Her husband, Bob, had deserted her two years ago to "pursue other interests." He left her two children to raise – eleven-year-old Kelly, and nine-year-old Daniel – and a mortgage that was now her burden. Hiking, golf, working out at the fitness club, cooking gourmet meals, even playing shortstop on the company's softball team — all the things she loved doing in her former life — had been put on the back burner, perhaps indefinitely. There was no time to squeeze these interests between her full-time job and full-time kids. Bob moved from Philadelphia to San Diego so she was on her own.

But her career? That was something she could count on! She found value in her success and knew her company and clients needed her. She needs to be needed. Lauren joined Dividend Enterprise Group (DEG) six years ago, in part due to her technical background and MBA in Finance fitting the needs of the firm, and in part because DEG appeared to be intent on encouraging — and

We're stronger than we think. empowering — women to climb the corporate ladder. At least that's what their website boasted. So when her boss, Richard Harper, delivered the news at last week's staff meeting that one of the "good ol' boys" had gotten the promotion she targeted, she felt as if she'd landed face down in the mud, knocked off a crazed rodeo bull.

Despite the beautiful spring weather, she drove home to College-ville from Center City that evening with her windows rolled up so she could scream. "It's not fair! It's not right! It's outrageous! Seriously? Peter is an idiot and does not deserve that promotion! I do! I-i-i-i-i-I do!" She wildly pounded her steering wheel while screeching to a halt at a red light.

Though he didn't graduate, Peter attended Boston University as had Richard. The two were longtime buddies. Peter had only been with the company for just over two years, and, in that time, he thoroughly demonstrated his overall ignorance and ineptitude. Lauren and several co-workers had surreptitiously nicknamed him "Peter Principle" because he'd been promoted twice to his next level of incompetence.[1] But Peter was just named Venture Partner, and Lauren was not. Yes, she was livid. Furious! Resentful and utterly

---

[1]The Peter Principle states that "in a hierarchy every employee tends to rise to his level of incompetence", meaning that employees tend to be promoted until they reach a position at which they cannot work competently. Dr. Laurence J. Peter and Raymond Hull formulated it in their 1969 book *The Peter Principle.*

disappointed. Her mood swung sharply the other direction as she turned off the 76 Interstate and onto the exit towards home. As she approached her beautiful neighborhood, trees dressed in early spring pink and white blossoms, with forsythia and lilacs just beginning to strut their stuff, Lauren eagerly looked forward to spending time with her kids. Sometimes they can be your best friends. *I really do have it good, and am grateful for what is so wonderful about my life. If only I could...*She shut down her thoughts on this challenging day as she shut down her phone, deciding not to think about work, and pulled into the driveway of her home.

Daughter Kelly was sitting at the kitchen table working on an art project.

"Where's your brother?" Lauren asked.

"Guess."

"X-Box?"

"Right. He's in his room glued to some stupid race car game."

"Well, maybe he's in training for his license," Lauren suggested as she went upstairs to Danny's room. "Scary thought," she mumbled.

Lauren knocked on Danny's door.

"Enter, racing fans," Danny responded in his deepest voice.

Despite her frustrating day, Lauren couldn't help laugh as she turned the knob of her son's bedroom door. "I'm home."

"I'm not. I'm in the greatest auto race on earth. And I'm winning." Danny's eyes were glued to his gaming console.

"Oh yeah," she challenged, "give me a controller. I know what to do behind the wheel. You shoulda seen me drive home tonight." They laughed.

Lauren tried to get Danny's attention. "What was the high point of your day?"

"Mom, I did this clay sculpture of an Uckron warrior in his battle armor, and the teacher said it was great!"

"She said it was great?"

"She said it was weird. That was good enough for me! "

"You just may change the world someday, young warrior. Did you have any lows?" Lauren asked.

"Well, kinda. I only got a 70 on my spelling test."

"Daniel Patrick, we worked on those words last night. You got them all correct."

"I know, Mom, but my brain don't like tests."

"Doesn't."

"Doesn't."

"Can you say the right word in a complete sentence?"

"My brain doesn't like tests."

Lauren turned her attention to Kelly, lingering in Danny's doorway. "How about you? Any highs and lows?"

"No lows, Mom. My day was great!" Kelly replied enthusiastically.

Lauren's curiosity was piqued. "What made it great?"

"There's a new boy in my class. He is SO cute!"

Danny nearly choked on his bubble gum, "Cute?"

Kelly blushed. "Well…um…I mean…he's…um…nice!"

Lauren smiled, Danny continued to choke, and Kelly was compelled to change the subject.

"How was your day, Mom?"

"Yeah, Mom," Danny chimed in. "What were your highs and lows?" Danny showed sincere interest, dropping his video game controller.

"It was just an average day. No special highs or lows." But then a lump grew in Lauren's throat and a tear in her eye slowly rolled down her cheek. "No, it wasn't average," she finally admitted. "There was a really low low."

Kelly wrapped her arms around her mom. "What's wrong, Mom? Is it something about Dad?

"No, it's not about Dad. It's about my job."

"What happened, Mom?"

With that, Lauren unraveled. She told her kids about the promotion, and how she didn't get it. And how Peter did. She told them about how this promotion could have been a miracle, and could have saved them from struggling to make the house payments or even having to downsize to a more affordable home. Then strong, independent, survivor Lauren Colton cried in her children's presence.

Both race-car champ Danny, and boy-crazy Kelly wrapped their arms around their mom.

"It will be all right," Kelly said.

"It will be, Mom," Danny confirmed, giving his mom the tightest hug ever.

Later that evening, exhausted, Lauren got in bed, with those affirmations fresh in her mind, somehow finding the energy to record her thoughts in her journal.

> *I can't believe how hard today was. I just wanted to hide under my desk. I feel so vulnerable. I could feel my shoulders slumped and my confidence zapped. I can't let this continue to show at work. I've got to dig deep and put on my game face. What's done is done. Guess I have to move on. It feels so unfair. What have I done wrong? I don't see it. I need a new strategy. At least I have to talk to Richard about what was in his mind. How did this happen? How did I miss this? Thank goodness for the blessing of two wonderful children.*

She put her journal back on the nightstand, took a deep breath, shut off the light, and rolled onto the far left of her bed as she did every night. *I wish my head could shut off like that light.*

Reflection and Analysis Generate Small Steps, BIG Gains

The disappointment of being passed over for a promotion can be a deal breaker for some. It seems unfair when former colleagues or friends are selected for key positions you feel *you* deserve.

Lauren experienced the Peter Principle first hand. The principle defines the common practice of promoting people to their highest level of incompetence. Said differently, just because you're good in one position (i.e., technical work) doesn't mean you'll be effective at the next level (i.e., managing people who do the technical work).

Who knows if Peter is, in fact, the right person for the job. All we know is Lauren wasn't chosen. The only thing she controls is how she responds to the news.

Create Your Own Five Degrees of Change

What is your high from today?

What is your low?

What setbacks have you had to overcome recently?

What process did you go through? Denial? Envy? Regret? Frustration?

With whom do you reflect about your day and thoughts?

With whom can you be vulnerable?

Rebound from Mistakes

"If the career you have chosen has some unexpected
inconvenience, console yourself by reflecting
that no career is without them."

— Jane Fonda
American Actress and Fitness Buff

Mistakes, fumbles, errors and screw-ups are part of playing the game of life and work. If you're going to fail is not the question. Everyone makes missteps and experiences mini-failure. How you rebound, guided by your attitude, and what actions you take are what matters most.

Lauren makes a common mistake. In haste, she emails the wrong person the wrong message. These things happen when we don't slow ourselves down long enough to think. Managing pace and anticipating the unexpected is a skill Lauren is developing…slowly.

❖ ❖ ❖

Lauren was pensive and feeling ambivalent about her situation as she drove into the city. She resolved to allot her forty-minute commute time to reviewing her current situation and challenges and how to face the day before her. The quiet evening with phone shut off, conversing and playing with her kids did her a world of good. Even the catharsis of writing in her journal seemed to help her sleep soundly through the night. *"A good night's sleep surely makes a difference in my attitude. A well-rested mind helps me realize how much I've been given. I know my life is not a complete failure."*

Determined to be cheerful and project this positive attitude, Lauren was upbeat as she entered the building. "Morning, James!" Everyone at DEG — and all the other building tenants — were acquainted with security guard James Whitaker's big smile and cheery greeting at the entrance security desk. There was just a certain something about that man that could instantly make people happy.

Lately Lauren seemed so down in the dumps. Her jovial greeting took him aback. "You're the first one in today from the management team, Ms. Colton," James offered with a wink. "How are those beautiful kids?"

Notice and appreciate the sources of wisdom in your life.

Lauren felt overcome by a deeper bond with James rather suddenly. "They're great, thanks for asking, James. Kelly seems to have a little crush, but the young man seems to run hot and cold. Some days he ignores her, some days he lights her up. Growing pains, right James?"

"Ah, yes indeed, Ms. Colton." James broke into a hearty laugh. "Life is full of meaningful lessons. Everyone must learn them. Plus it helps to see the good in these trials. It makes it worth the pain."

Lauren looked back at James for a moment. She tried to put aside the thoughts of Richard and Bob that were rushing through her mind. "You're sure right about that. Enjoy the day, James." "Sure will," he replied, "you do the same."

Lauren popped off the elevator, grabbing a quick peak out the DEG office lobby window at the historic city of Philadelphia and the sun's reflection on the Delaware River. One look at that awesome view reminded her to be grateful for all the good in her life. She glanced at the stylish Cartier watch Bob gave her right before he left. Sometimes the watch depressed her, but this time, she could somehow just admire its simplistic sweeping elegance.

Lauren adjusted her heavy laptop shoulder bag and straightened her pencil skirt, purposefully striding down the hallway. Today was a day to put her intentions on savoring and enjoyment, not to dwell on negatives. She smiled proudly as she thought about the talented pool of diverse individuals she'd hired and brought together, ruminating briefly on their accomplishments as a group and as individuals. Despite this recent missed-promotion setback, there was a lot to feel fortunate for, both at work and at home.

She swung open her office door so quickly, papers flew off of her desk. Without blinking or thinking, she fired up her laptop and read the Wall Street Journal headlines.

Trusted colleague Sohan Budrick popped his head into her door. "Good morning. How was your night?"

"Hey, Sohan," she said brightly. "My night was awesome! I refused to work, turned off my phone and just hung out with the kids. It felt so liberating to just do what I wanted. Not what I typically do at night: work. You know?"

"It's great you're taking better care of your physical and emotional well-being. In the end, it will serve you well and you'll accomplish more in your day. I'm off to brew up some green tea. Want to join me?" Sohan was a yoga devotee whose lifestyle was far too healthy for anyone in venture capital.

"Thanks for the offer. I need to get a couple of things done before Richard's staff meeting, but I'll definitely take a rain check."

"I'll keep that in mind," Sohan offered warmly.

As she hovered over the credenza, she watched 51 new email messages upload since she'd checked her iPhone before leaving her house. One from her pal Paul Nolan was marked urgent.

Paul wrote:

"Hey. Sorry to hear about yesterday. You're a much more talented financier than Peter. What happened? Drop me a line when you get the chance."

Lauren drafted a quick response to Paul. "Apparently I'm working at a firm that values fraternity friends over results. Found out Peter and his brother Thomas are Richard's good college buddies. Thanks for the support. I appreciate it. Today I'm feeling good for a change."

She hit send. Lauren never noticed that the email address default picked up the "P" in Peter instead of Paul Nolan. Message sent.

❖ ❖ ❖

Richard's meetings seldom started on time. It was universally understood that a 9:30 a.m. meeting would begin at least 15 to 30 minutes late. Lauren had long ago adjusted her internal clock to account for Richard time. She finished up some last-minute research and walked into the conference room at 9:45. Everyone was there, including Richard, and the meeting had already begun. Lauren quietly slid into a seat at the table.

"Thanks for joining us, Lauren," Richard smirked. His singsong tone was clearly condescending and sarcastic.

"Sorry I'm late. I didn't expect the meeting to start on time," Lauren said, defensively.

"It's a 9:30 meeting," he retorted. Smiling at the rest of the team and with direct, stern eye contact, Richard said, "Let's chat offline."

Lauren didn't share her research. In fact, she didn't speak at all or change her facial expression. She was disheartened — physically present but mentally disconnected from the boardroom. Repeatedly reviewing recent conversations drowned out the voices of her co-workers. *What did I say, what did I do that so obviously darkened Richard's attitude towards me?* She had arrived at work and at the meeting feeling great and ready to make things happen, yet everything seemed to crash in the blink of an eye.

How quickly things can change.

When the meeting adjourned, stomach in knots, Lauren made her way down to Richard's corner office. Generally Richard would greet her with a welcoming smile, but today he simply said, "Shut the door."

Oh, *crap!* was the only thought that came to Lauren's mind.

"I'm extremely disappointed," Richard said angrily.

"I don't know what you're talking about, Richard."

"Yeah, well, a recent email exchange indicates you have a problem with decisions coming from my office, like Peter's promotion. It was a decision senior leadership and the board strategically made. Would you like to request we review our decision again, Lauren?"

Richard was hot. Really hot. Lauren had seen his anger before, but never had she been on the receiving end. Caught off guard, she fumbled for words.

"Well, I—"

"We had a conversation about this when the decision was in the process of being made. I explained that you're not ready for this role, Lauren. You're good, but you're not as qualified as Peter. Don't make this decision about him instead of you. I saw the email you sent accidentally to Peter — you need to be more careful about voicing your opinions."

Lauren had no idea she'd sent her rant to the wrong party and couldn't wait to research her sent messages. She was beyond embarrassed, mortified at her mistake, flustered, and sure it showed. She took a deep breath, and despite all the excuses and apologies she thought to voice, decided it best to keep her response impersonal and professional.

"I know you want me to increase all gross margins to over fifty percent, but I don't know how I can find Market Leaders without being Venture Partner. It's just not possible."

"You'll figure it out — or you'll have other things to figure out."

A mental alarm sounded in Richard's head, triggered by Human Resources as he uttered these rather explosive words. He decided it best to soften his stance. "Don't get all upset about this stuff, Els. **Play nice with others.** You're doing great. We'll get you a Venture Partner title soon enough. Trust me, it will all work out." Richard turned his chair toward the window, a clear indicator that the conversation had come to an end.

Questions and comments raced through Lauren's head. Not quite knowing what would be appropriate to actually say or ask aloud, she settled on keeping her mouth shut. Her mind was racing and she felt as though she was having an out-of-body experience.

Imposter Syndrome: Despite external evidence of their competence, those with the syndrome remain convinced that they are frauds and do not deserve the success they have achieved.

The person playing along was not she but a parody of herself. It was getting harder and harder to discern where the real Lauren ended and the "corporate" Lauren started.

Lonely and uncertain, Lauren raced out of Richard's office looking for somewhere to hide. *What do I do now?* Her heart was sinking and she was struck by a sense of purposelessness. Cheerful and positive flew out the window. However, rather than give the incident much thought, Lauren quickly returned to the notion of getting busy to drown out the negative noise.

Reflection and Analysis Generate Small Steps, BIG Gains

Well, "the best laid plans of mice and men"…is certainly a truism. Things can and often do go awry. One somewhat impulsive, non-reflective email pulled the rug out from under what Lauren planned to be a bright, brave day of confidence and competence.

What can we glean from this event in Lauren's day that will move her and us forward? A multitude of opportunities, options and decisions, most unplanned, are presented to us each day. There

Focus equals results.

are many directions we can take. Our first step is to identify our *focus*. With her statement "…at least my life isn't a complete failure. There is really so much else wonderful about it," Lauren demonstrated a focus on committing to being cheerful and positive. What happened? Forgetting her commitment to and focus on projecting positivity, Lauren crafted a negative-sounding email response to Paul's pure, simple "drop me a line when you get a chance." Worse yet, her haste resulted in the ultimately costly move of sending the email to the wrong person. And, when Richard revealed her emailing error, she felt as if her world was falling apart. Lauren forgot her focus on her commitment to remain positive. Perhaps she could demonstrate her focus on and commitment to positivity by making light of the email gaffe while in Richard's presence, and leave with a determination to make the best of the situation. If the best-laid plans for you, Lauren and me can and do go awry, we can only try to keep our spirits high, shrug it off, learn from our mistakes, and move forward.

It's essential to prepare for important meetings, conversations, and presentations. We must not only mentally prepare the message we intend to deliver, but also the method of delivery and the impact we aim to have. We must also remember our focus. Given the luxury of advance notice, (i.e. a budget presentation to the team next month) we have time to craft the message, the appropriate language we can use to express ourselves, and the way we want to dress and deliver the message.

But as noted, even our best-laid plans can be challenged by day-to-day life realities. What about impromptu and unexpected interactions? Regardless of the circumstances, three factors help us redirect from what is, to what is desired. These include: **Focus, View and Action**.

Focus, view and action.

Focus: As evidenced in your life and Lauren's story, each moment provides numerous demands for our attention. It is essential to ask, answer, and hold true to our answer to the question, "What will I focus on?" Be selective and intentional.

View: Everyone views his or her own life through personal prisms. As such, discerning and interpreting the objective realities of any one moment can be challenging and filled with bias and distortion. We must step back and reflect on the question, "How can I take the 'I' out of this situation to see it more objectively?" "How is my perspective influencing my interpretation of what's happening?"

Action: Considering our chosen focus, we need to quickly assess the available options – and commit to what will most likely move us forward. Lauren needed to pause and ask, "Given my focus for today, how and when will I respond to Paul's email?" Having asked that question and the implied "what action will I take?" may have saved her the pain of this careless mistake.

Create Your Own Five Degrees of Change

You're *busy*. Everyone is! But achieving our goals takes more than good intentions or wishful thinking. There is so much to learn and so much to do. But as noted throughout this book, the most successful approach is guided by small steps…five degrees at a time…that will result in BIG Gains.

Take a moment to reflect on each of the following. Write down your responses. Commit to acting on at least one of your insights.

- Think of a time when you "showed up" the way you intended. You managed something well and delivered the message flawlessly. What enabled your effectiveness?
- Do you recall what you focused on?
- What was your perspective of the situation and your performance?
- What action did you take?
- How about a time that *didn't* go so well?
- What did you *focus* on?
- What was your *view* of the situation?
- What *action* did you take?
- Last, how can you remind yourself to *always* proof emails and distribution lists before hitting send?

Additional Resources

Koval, R. & Thaler-Kaplan, L. (2007). The Power of Nice: How to conquer the business world with kindness. Crown Business. 2006.

Canfield, J., Hansen, M.V. & Hewitt, L. (2000). The Power of Focus. Health Communications, Inc. 2000.

Dawn Michelle Baude. The Executive Guide to E-mail Correspondence: Including Model Letters for Every Situation. Career Press. 2006.

Expect the Unexpected

> *"You gain strength, courage and confidence by every experience in which you really stop to look fear in the face...You must do the thing you cannot do."*
>
> —Eleanor Roosevelt
> *First Lady and Civil Rights Advocate*

What do we do to recover from mistakes and problems born of our carelessness? What choice do we have? We can passively shove those mistakes under the rug, hoping they miraculously disappear. Or, face the fire and courageously correct the problem. When unexpected interactions occur, it's easy to personalize the communication, not see the bigger picture, see the cup half empty, and get brain freeze and tongue-tied, or put one's foot in one's mouth. Improvising an on-the-spot, effective communication when life takes the unanticipated turn *is* challenging. Times like these require us to summon our courage, stay cool and confident, be mature and thoughtful. In

Don't take things personally.

the workplace, we have to take care to be particularly professional, even when those communicating to us seem to be doing so from left field. Expecting the unexpected is the only way to retain our personal power and continue as an effective participant in the creative process.

Lauren is sick about the email error and Richard's disappointment with her unprofessional carelessness. She's determined to set the record straight. Then she's caught by surprise by a whole new turn of events. What can we learn from how she reacts to these circumstances?

❖ ❖ ❖

Lauren must have punched the snooze button on her iPod alarm clock radio six or seven times before she finally ventured out of bed. It usually only took a few bars of music to get her going. But she knew today would be different. She'd apologize to her boss Richard and try to ask the huge question she was well aware could get her fired: *what is the* real *reason I didn't get the promotion?*

In an effort to balance assertiveness and an appropriate apology with indignation and regret for her email faux pas, she reviewed and rehearsed a proper approach during her office commute.

"Richard, I'm sorry for the careless email to Paul."

"Richard, the email to Paul was careless. I'm really sorry." "No, just I'm sorry."

"I shouldn't have sent that email to Paul. Careless mistake."

Stunned and aghast when Richard informed her about his decision to promote Peter instead of her, Lauren never initiated a discussion with him. On one hand, she could kick herself for not taking the bull by the horns when the opportunity presented itself yesterday to confront the matter right then and there. On the other, now that she had time to sleep on it, she felt better prepared to apologize and discuss why Peter was promoted. By the time she parked the car, Lauren was nervous, but nevertheless determined...and ready.

Lauren walked into the DEG executive suite and approached Ms. Hard-Nosed Executive Assistant, Ethel. "May I see Richard? I just need three minutes."

"He's not here yet," Ethel was curt.

Typical. Richard expects us to be on time every day — not even a minute late — but he strolls in whenever he feels like it. Not much of a leadership example.

"Mind if I wait?"

"Not at all. Could be awhile, though. I think he's at the club."

Lauren took a seat across from Ethel and replied to email with her phone. Twenty-five minutes later, Richard arrived.

Though Lauren was seated not more than twelve feet away, Richard appeared not to notice her. "Hi, Ethel. Any messages?"

"A few, mostly emails. Nothing really important."

"Good! I'm not in the mood for anything important yet." Richard laughed as he walked toward his office.

"Oh, Mr. Harper. Ms. Colton is here to see you."

Richard turned back to see Lauren. "Sorry, Els, I didn't see you."

Els? I still can't figure out why he calls me 'Els,' thought Lauren.

"Please come in. I've been looking forward to talking to you."

Lauren's face shifted from calm to concern. *What does he want to talk to me about,* she thought, with knots in her stomach as she followed Richard into his beautifully appointed office overlooking Philadelphia's most magnificent views of the Delaware River and beyond.

"Sit down. Please. Be comfortable."

Lauren slid into the overstuffed leather chair nearest his massive lacquered walnut desk.

"I know why you're here," said Richard without missing a beat. "You're probably upset about yesterday and mostly that you didn't get the Venture Partner position. Am I right?"

With Richard diving in so quickly, appearing to innately knowing her mind, Lauren was once again caught off-guard, all her carefully rehearsed statements suddenly inaccessible. "Well, I have to admit it took me by —"

"When I'm right, I'm right, correct?"

Expect the unexpected.

"I…um…I don't know how to say this, Richard, but I'm really sorry about the email and think — rather, *know* — I'm more qualified for the position than Peter. I've been here longer. I know a great deal more about the process and the system. I know the clients, the pro forma, what makes this company money. And I think I've proven it several times over."

"True enough, Els. You've proven a lot of things. But not enough to warrant *that position*. When it comes to your role within the company, work still needs to be done. Peter has potential to get up to speed quickly. He understands our business and has a strong network. He has a good grip on digital and social media and will bring some fresh ideas."

Coaching is an investment companies make to retain and develop valuable talent.

Lauren was stunned. "I'm sorry. I don't understand."

Richard could be blunt and to the point, especially with topics that made him uncomfortable. He panicked about anything related to, or verging on, what might become or be perceived as a personnel issue. "I'll cut to the chase. We're hiring a coach for you. Someone to work with you and help you with whatever is getting in your way. I think it'll be good for you. A coach'll be able to give you advice and perspective."

I had the feeling Lauren would come to me first, Richard mused. She's a strong-willed gal, who stands her ground and can be a true asset to us. Her tenacity is actually one of her best qualities in a work environment highly charged with forceful masculine energy like ours. But our greatest strengths can also be our greatest weaknesses. Approach and discernment are areas in which Lauren needs a little refinement and shaping, but she's got the basics. She's smart, savvy, and has good instincts about where we should be investing. But she's overdramatic and in her head far too much.

"Really." Lauren knew her steely, one-word response came off cold, even inappropriate, but she couldn't help herself. In the blink of an eye, her shoulders tensed and her arms folded slowly in front of her chest.

"Hey, Els. Please. Don't get defensive. Investing in a coach for your development should show you how much we value you as a vital human capital asset. We want to take care of you. Besides, it'll help you rebound from this whole promotion thing. It's obvious you're taking it hard."

Lauren could feel color rising up into her neck and face. She felt like a ticking time bomb, fearful she might burst into tears or explode into expletives — neither of which would enhance her career. She worked hard to keep her emotions under control. "I'm really fine, Richard. Trust me."

"Glad you're on board, Els. It's going to be good for you. Just a 'thanks' is sufficient." Richard winked. "Andrea Lombardi is the name of your coach. Coach Lombardi will call later today." Richard roared at his humorous reference to Vince Lombardi, the former Green Bay Packers' coach. Underneath his jocular exterior, Richard was actually quite sensitive.

Lauren's totally worth it. I've worked with coach Lombardi in the past and know she can manage Lauren's intellect and energy to help foster appropriate positive changes by finding the simplest common denominators, helping her clients one small step at a time. I'm confident Andrea's techniques will help Lauren mature and make some essential personal changes that will help us forge ahead gracefully in this ever-changing marketplace.

Assuming the meeting was over, Lauren stood up to leave. "Ummm…I'll look forward to Andrea's call." She decided it would be a bad choice to balk at Richard's directive or question him about becoming Venture Partner.

"Speaking of coaching and training and all…are you planning to get back running with us at lunch?" Richard asked. "You haven't been out there in months."

"Err, well, if I get a chance —"

"Great. We're going to do three miles today around noon. Meet us downstairs at the gym. Oh, one last quick thing. Get me that business plan analysis for the new IT startup we discussed yesterday. I need to review it before the management meeting at 10:00 this morning."

Lauren rushed to her office, firmly shut the door, and sank into her chair. Her head was pounding. *What on earth was that? A coach?*

Seriously? My career is moving backwards, not forward. This is a joke. Focus, Lauren, focus. Now, where did I save that business plan? Vigorously trying to shove her feelings down into a dark place and focus instead on what was comfortable — work — Lauren shook her head. Her eyes landed on the dusty gym bag, knowing — again — there was little chance of making it to the lunch run. *I can't wait for this day to be over. Maybe running will help clear my head. I wish I could just climb into bed. Is getting a coach a good thing? It's like one step away from termination, right? What a mess.*

Reflection and Analysis Generate
Small Steps, BIG Gains

Preparation is critical to success, and expecting the unexpected is equally essential. Considering "what if" scenarios helps maintain focus, especially when courageous conversations don't go as planned. Lauren is thrown off by Richard's comment about looking forward to speaking with her, and loses concentration on her intent and desired outcome for the conversation. Defensiveness and self-protection disrupt clear vision. Lauren's desire was to be assertive. She diligently prepared to be clear, professional and strong. Then, when confronted with surprising news about receiving a coach, Lauren relinquishes her power, becoming insecure and weak. She loses focus of her intent and doesn't resist the temptation to take the bait of distraction – the unexpected. Five degree shifts that would help Lauren include: having a visual reminder of her goal or outcome to stay focused, asking a good question to get more information about the surprising news or simply expressing appreciation and recognizing her personal power to create a new empowering meaning.

Create Your Own Five Degrees of Change

Courageous conversations require preparation. You must consider what the other may say, anticipate the quality of the exchange and clarify – in advance – your desired outcome. What should you say? What shouldn't you say? Prepare, and unlike Lauren who got caught off guard, have Plan B ready in case the conversation takes an unexpected turn, gets postponed, has a distraction or an element that compromises your focused intention.

Record your answers to these questions to prepare for your next courageous conversation or confrontation.

- What is the goal of the communication? On what must you focus?
- Do you want to build rapport? If so, how?
- Do you want to get information? If yes, what do you need to know?
- What specific outcome must you accomplish in this conversation?
- What must you *not* focus on? What anxiety, fear, negative feelings, distractions, and insecurities do you need to block during this conversation?
- How are you going to express your point of view?
- What words and phrases best express what you mean?
- What's the appropriate tone and pace for this conversation?
- What words or phrases should you *avoid*?
- Since body language is 55% of your message[2], how do you want to "show up"?
  - Posture
  - Eye contact
  - Breathing
  - Nonverbal gestures

Beware not to sabotage your success.

How Messages Are Received

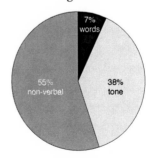

7% words

55% non-verbal

38% tone

---

[2]Albert Mehrabian, Professor Emeritus of Psychology, UCLA, published a study on the relative importance of verbal and nonverbal messages. His findings are known as the 7%-38%-55% rule. 7% words, 38% tone and 55% non-verbal.

Additional Resources

Pachter, B. and Magee, S. The Power of Positive Confrontation: The Skills You Need to Know to Handle Conflicts at Work, at Home and in Life. DaCapo Press. 2001

Patterson, K., et al. Crucial Conversations: Tools for Talking When Stakes Are High, Second Edition. McGraw-Hill, 2011.

Tannen, D. Talking from 9 to 5: Women and Men at Work. William Morrow Paperbacks, 1995.

Wydro, K. Think On Your Feet: The Art Of Thinking And Speaking Under Pressure. Simon and Schuster. 1981.

Prioritizing Priorities

"The key is not to prioritize what's on your schedule but to schedule your priorities."

—Stephen R. Covey
Leadership Authority and Best Selling Author

Actions speak louder than words. It's easy to say family is number one, good health is vital, and saving money is wise. But investing time and making progress in those areas takes targeted discipline and healthy habits of body, mind and spirit.

Lauren's habits include putting her work ahead of her time for Kelly and Danny. She struggles to find the balance between commitment to her career and time for her children.

◆ ◆ ◆

After dinner that evening Lauren was pooped but had emails to catch up on. She picked up her laptop and headed to her room. "Kids please clean up the kitchen, I've got to get some work done." Danny called after her. "Mom, wait! You promised you'd help me with my project for the science fair."

"Yes, Danny, you're right, I did. I promise we'll work on it tomorrow."

"But, Mom, the science fair *is* tomorrow. You said you'd help, and you said you'd come, too."

Immersed in her career concerns, Lauren had forgotten about Danny's project. She knew nothing about miniature radio-controlled airborne surveillance devices but she did know spelling — and how to use the dictionary function on her computer. At least she could help Danny be more articulate. *Where does this kid get all these wild ideas,* she wondered as she helped design and spell-check his charts.

When the project was finished around 10:30, Danny asked what time she'd make it to the fair. "Danny, honey, I'm not sure I'll make it. I have a big day at work tomorrow."

Danny's face fell but it was clear he was valiantly trying to hide his disappointment. "That's okay. It's not a big deal. Thanks for helping me. 'Night, Mom."

"Don't be up late. Brush teeth. PJs. Turn off all the lights," Lauren recited the bedtime reminders as she headed up the stairs.

Mom of the Year? Nope. | "Okay, Mom."

His sweet voice saddened her. The kids are so tolerant of her limited attention and constant tendency to choose work over all else. Her head was full of noise. She craved the catharsis of journaling her deepest thoughts.

Though he tried so hard to hide it, Danny looked so discouraged when I said I might not make it to the fair. I know he wants me there. I'm the worst mom on Earth. And this whole thing about a coach. Really! What will a coach tell me that I don't already know? She'll probably be some psychiatrist who will prove once and for all that I'm out of my mind. I'm such a loser. Not effective at work. Not effective at home. I'm a real masterpiece, I tell ya.

Mom of the Year? Nope. Not this year. My kids get scraps of my attention. It's a miracle they're as good as they are. I feel like such a failure. I'm at an all-time low. My mortgage is more than I can afford, I am going nowhere at work, I've got to speak to a business therapist and my kids need me more than ever. I don't know what to do. I'm done. Out of energy. Out of ideas.

Lauren put down her journal and gently she knocked on Danny's door, opened it a crack, and peeked in to see if he was awake. He lay still in his bed. She walked in and sat down next to him.

"I'm sorry, honey," she said tenderly, stroking his hair.

"It's okay," he sniffled.

"It's *not* okay and I'm *really* sorry. I'll figure out a way to get to your science fair tomorrow. I'll reschedule some meetings and make it happen, okay?"

"Thanks, Mom." Danny wiped his eyes and sat up to hug Lauren.

Reflection and Analysis Generate Small Steps, BIG Gains

The only way to really connect with others is to make a commitment to spending quality time with them. The scarcest resource available today is attention. There are so many ways distractions vie for your attention. Give the people you love some quality time. Don't multitask them.

The scarcest resource available today is attention.

Lauren trusted her instincts and sat with Danny to apologize and commit to him. She made him a priority, something he really needed. She committed to him, knowing it would be a promise difficult to keep.

Stephen Covey (1996) tells a great story about the things to which we should devote our time. It starts with a time management instructor quizzing his students about fitting rocks into a big glass gallon jar. He put large rocks in and asked the students if the jar was full. They said yes. He then pulled out a bucket of gravel and put it in. The students again thought it was full. The instructor poured in sand and then water until the jar was full to the brim.

If you don't put the big rocks in first, you'll never get them in at all.

One student explained that the moral of the story is you can fit more in and do more than you think. The professor corrected the assumption. "The truth this illustration teaches us is that if you don't put the big rocks in first, you'll never get them in at all."

The shift is to know what your big rocks are and put them into your life first. Don't leave the best for last.

Create Your Own Five Degrees of Change

Record your answers to these questions —

1. What are your life's big rocks? Your children, your loved ones, your education, your dreams, a worthy cause, teaching others, doing things that you love, your health, your mate?
2. How much do you invest in those things?
3. What new routine or habit will remind you to put these *big rocks* into your schedule first?
4. What will you have to give up to make space for what matters most?

Additional Resources

Covey, S., Merrill, A.R., Merrill, R. First Things First. Free Press. 1996

Ruiz, D. and Wilton, N. The Four Agreements: A Practical Guide to Personal Freedom. Amber-Allen Publishing. 2011

Say No To Say Yes to the Right Things

"Each of us, every waking hour, is called upon to say no, whether to friends or family members, to our bosses, employees, or co-workers, or to ourselves. Whether and how we say no determines the very quality of our lives. It is perhaps the most important word to learn to say gracefully and effectively."

—William Ury

Mediator, Writer and Negotiation Expert

Lauren is paying closer attention to messages and signs to help her better understand how to make improvements in her life. She begins to realize one pattern that may be causing pain. That's the habit of agreeing to be "all things" at work at the price of what matters most.

◆ ◆ ◆

As Lauren listened to National Public Radio during her commute, she transitioned to a more focused head space. The NPR host was interviewing negotiation expert Dr. William Ury, best-selling author of *Getting to Yes* and *Getting Past No,* and other popular books. Dr. Ury spoke about the power of a positive no. "When you say 'no' to something in your life, that 'no' is almost always grounded in a bigger 'yes.' For example, if I'm scheduled to do something with my family and an opportunity at work comes along — I say 'no' to the new opportunity because I'm saying 'yes' to the original one. It's like that with negotiations and many other things in life. We have to say no to certain things to say yes to what matters most."

'No' is almost always grounded in a bigger 'yes'.

Lauren thought this over as it applied to her life. She did have a tendency to say yes to practically anything at work but often say no to the kids. At work, she suffered from "FOMO"— the Fear Of Missing Out. If there was a committee, a task force, a special sub-committee, even a birthday cake group needing volunteers, Lauren felt compelled to raise her hand.

If I apply Ury's concepts to my home and job lives, I won't need a coach, she told herself.

NPR went to station ID and promo. Lauren's thoughts turned toward her frustration about being passed up for the promotion. *Her* promotion. The one she felt promised in her last review. She'd earned it, having always delivered whatever was asked of her, always eagerly volunteering to take on more. As she pulled onto the off-ramp, she mused, *What's my bigger yes? Am I really able to always sort out what matters most, focus on it, and not say yes when I should be saying no?*

Reflection and Analysis Generate Small Steps, BIG Gains

Agreeing to help out a new employee, volunteering to organize the birthday of the month initiative, or staying late to complete a project due tomorrow seem to be "good" things to do. Without context, it's impossible to judge if these are *good*

"Who pays the price for my choices?"

or not. Often we say "yes" to fill a deeper need – for example, a need to belong, or simply a need to be *needed*. We must always take an honest look at what we commit to and not express a willingness aloud to others to make that commitment, unless we have some certainty that we can follow through and not over-extend ourselves. Someone always ends up paying the price if we over-index on commitments in one area of our life – work, for example. Someone may pay the price for my choice to commit. If we over-index on commitments in one area of life, like work, we must honestly ask ourselves: "*Who pays the price for my choices?*" You pay by losing investments in your family, friends and other interests. They pay the price too. Nearly all of us have too many things to do at any given time. One must constantly weigh, choose carefully, and try to retain a balance, challenging though it may be. Saying "yes" to the things you value most will strengthen you to say "no" when the price for "yes" is too costly.

Create Your Own Five Degrees of Change

All you get is twenty-four hours in your day. Make sure you get everything you want out of those hours for yourself, your career, and your loved ones. Use the spreadsheet below to categorize how you will organize the demands on your time.

Saying no can be awkward, guilt inducing, nerve-racking, embarrassing, and even risky to your friendships and career. In his books *Getting to Yes* and *Getting Past No*, Ury says, " 'No' may be the most powerful word in the language, but it's also potentially the most destructive, which is why it's hard to say."[3] Ury

> **'No' may be the most powerful word.**

offers guidance in his book on how to tactfully deal with situations in which you simply want to say no. Ury shares that no is tough to say because it highlights the tension between claiming one's personal power and tending to personal relationships — a need to keep everyone happy. Often people respond on either side of the spectrum, putting too much emphasis on minimizing conflict by saying yes when they really want to say no — or by saying no in a rough way and bruising the recipient.

---

[3] The Power of a Positive No: How to Say No and Still Get to Yes, Dr. William Ury

The better option, according to Ury, is to *provide the "No" between two yeses.* For example, when asked to work late on a Friday night, say "Yes"! to your own interests (value family), then move on to your "No". (I will not work late tonight), and finish up by saying "Yes"? to your employer's needs - suggest an alternative option (How can we get the work done without my staying late tonight?) Notice the punctuation: **Yes!** (to your values) **No.** (to the request) **Yes?** (to your recommended solution).

Writing goals significantly increases liklihood of accomplishing them.

Although we may intuitively understand the importance of saying "No", we often don't because of the dozen "what ifs" that come to mind. Ury says that in a world with more information, more relationships, and ever-increasing demands on our time, individuals must be able to say "No" in a productive way. The bottom line is, saying "No" really means saying "Yes"! to the right things.

Process for clearing your head and organizing your thoughts:

- Set a timer for two minutes.
- Brain dump everything that's on your mind (thoughts, goals, tasks) onto paper. Handwritten is best, but typing works too.
- Write down your goals
- List your commitments and your role (i.e. boss, peer, parent)
- Stop after two minutes.
- Put a check mark next to the items you must say "Yes"! to.
- Cross out what you need to say "No" to.
- Put someone else's initials next to something you will delegate.
- If you're not sure, put a question mark to indicate it's something you still need to decide. It's something for the future and you'll need to think about it again, but not right now.

You must cross off *at least one thing* to say "No" to in order to say "Yes"! to yourself!

To Do, To Don't, To Delegate

TO DO	TO DON'T	TO DELEGATE	TO DECIDE

Additional Resources

Ury, W. The Power of a Positive No: How to Say No and Still Get to Yes, Bantam, 2007

Breitman, P. and Hatch, C. How to Say No Without Feeling Guilty: And Say Yes to More Time, and What Matters Most to You. Broadway. 2001

Robinson, D. Too Nice for Your Own Good: How to Stop Making 9 Self-Sabotaging Mistakes. Grand Central Publishing. 2000

Look For Blind Spots

"What I am looking for is not out there, it is in me."

—Helen Keller

American Author and Lecturer

auren is about to meet her coach. She's anxious about what it means to be selected for executive coaching and if and how coaching can help her career. She feels like a failure and needs new perspective and resilience to bounce back from her negative reaction to coaching. She views it as remedial and a last ditch effort before her position is eliminated. The uncertainty she has about coaching seems to outweigh any possible benefits she could reap. Lauren has her sight, yet she suffers from limited vision. She has blind spots as she struggles to see beyond herself, her needs and her perspective. It will help to have another set of eyes on the situation.

Lauren parked her car in a spot closest to the entrance, noticing Peter's name on a newly-updated sign posted in front of one of the top executives' reserved parking spaces in the parking garage. *What an insult.*

"Morning, Ms. Colton!"

"Morning, James." Lauren's forced smile could be seen a mile away.

"Excuse me, Ms. Colton. It's none of my business, but you were in such good spirits when I last saw you but not so much today. Everything all right?"

"I'm sorry, James. I'm afraid that lately life has been a real roller coaster."

"You got whatever you need already."

"Whatever it is, Ms. Colton, know you *got* whatever you need already."

"Thanks James." However grateful for her friend, Lauren was distracted, nervously aware she was already a bit late, and ever so conscious that today was the day "The Coach" would enter her life.

Lauren could hear James's voice in the distance, as the elevator doors were about to shut. "Don't forget to make time for your beautiful kids. You know they're a total blessing." Thoughts of Danny's science project and the fair gave her a rush of anxiety. *How am I going to keep my promise?*

◆   ◆   ◆

Like her gym bag beside the file cabinet and the huge piles of unread investor publications atop it, Lauren felt carelessly tossed aside and faded from years of unappreciated service. Her standard issue windowless office and dusty fake Ficus tree in its corner reinforced her feelings of being washed up, washed over. Again, she mused about her loss of the Venture

Am I not political enough?

Partner position. *Is it because I'm a woman? Am I not political enough? Why did Peter get to be Venture Partner? Richard said he had so much potential. Don't I have even more potential? I still don't feel I have all the answers to why Peter got the promotion instead of me.*

In trying to find some sense of value, Lauren busied herself with a variety of tasks. She pulled out contents of a client file and started examining the ROI (Return on Investment), opened the attachments her colleague Todd sent the night before and, while printing, scanned and replied to a dozen of her 89 new emails.

Lauren thought she excelled at multi-tasking – one more reason she truly believed she was among the team's most productive members.

Her thoughts ran to how her life would be different starting today — had she not lost the promotion to Peter. She'd be sitting in the office with a view of downtown Philadelphia, and a conference table with comfy chairs to accommodate other staffers at meetings. She learned some time ago in yoga classes she took for a short while how the right sort of breathing can help change your stuck pattern and allow you to focus deliberately on the present moment. Lauren took a slow deep breath, held it for the same length of time, then slowly exhaled, attempting to shift her focus away from self to the task at hand: getting things done. Suddenly her iPhone caught her attention. It was a text from friend Suzie, her former DEG colleague. Fed up with the company, Suzie ventured out on her own last year.

"OMG I just heard about what Richard did to you! The nerve. Peter? Really? Insane; the whole thing is crazy. Come work with me. Let's have lunch this week!"

Lauren deleted Suzie's message. She was a good friend to understand how horribly Lauren had been treated. But Suzie's negativity could be draining. *I'll call her later this afternoon if I can. I can barely make time for my kids. Friends need to wait. Sweet of her to think of me, though.*

Lauren's loyal admin Sylvia, with her since the firm opened, interrupted her thoughts. Ready to climb the ladder with her supervisor, Sylvia was nearly as disappointed by Peter's promotion as Lauren. "Lauren, there is an Andrea Lombardi here to see you. She says she has an appointment with you."

"She does, thank you, Sylvia."

A professionally-dressed woman greeted Lauren. As she extended her hand and smiled, Lauren was overwhelmed with embarrassment.

Lauren glanced at her reflection in the blackened computer screen. *Why do I need a coach? Why didn't I wear something nicer today? Did I remember to put on make-up? Has Richard told the rest of the company about this? Did everyone know she'd been singled out for 'special help?'* Lauren was justifiably skeptical of Richard's motives. She'd learned over the past few years about the hidden agenda behind altruistic acts, finding it hard to accept that Richard really wanted what was best for her. What was this coaching thing *really* about? And, her filled-to-the brim days didn't leave much time to hang with some feel-good coach.

"Andrea Lombardi," said the coach brightly as she introduced herself and extended a hand. "Nice to meet you."

"Nice to meet you, Andrea. Please have a seat." Lauren gestured to an available chair. "I have to ask you something kind of strange."

"Sure," Andrea pulled a notepad from her brown leather briefcase.

"Any chance you're related to the long-time Green Bay Packers Coach, Vince Lombardi?" Lauren instantly regretted asking such a juvenile question.

"No, sorry. Different kind of coach, different kind of coaching, different game altogether, though the purpose is the same. To help you succeed."

"Got it." Lauren nodded.

"Are those your kids?" Andrea studied the pictures on Lauren's bookshelf.

"Yes, Daniel is nine, Kelly is eleven." Lauren shied away from discussing her personal life at work, especially with strangers. It was easier to compartmentalize her personal and professional lives.

How many lives do you have? One.

Lauren observed her visitor intently, trying to discern how to position herself and make a favorable impression. "Can I get you anything? Water? Coffee?"

"I'm good, thanks. Time is precious so let's get started. I'm not sure how much you already know about the scope of our engagement. Please tell me what Richard has shared with you so I can answer any questions and help paint the picture of how we will work together."

"Blank canvas. He didn't tell me much. He has misinterpreted some of my stress lately and decided that I need *therapy* or something." Lauren didn't want to seem defensive or share too much personal information.

"How familiar are you with coaching?"

Due diligence for executive failures, she thought." To tell you the truth, not very. My neighbor is a senior executive at Comcast and often talks about her coach. She's had a positive experience and just got more responsibility but I don't know much about it, how it works, what we'll be doing together, what we'll talk about, how often we'll meet and for how much time. I'm guessing you're here to help me do a complete one-eighty."

"A one-eighty?"

"You know…like a 180-degree turn. Transform me from the way I do things to the way Richard — I mean DEG — wants me to be."

"No, that's not it at all. The key to a successful coaching relationship is that we make *incremental* changes. Instead of trying to do a 'one-eighty,' as you describe, we'll look at the small things on which you can build. Think of changing five degrees at a time."

> **Changing five degrees at a time.**

"So you're not here to help me fix all my weaknesses?"

"No. Not at all. Our work is about sharpening and polishing. Let's call what we'll work on 'The Five Degree Principle.' You're already successful. You're not broken. And in reality, *you* have to invite and allow any changes that might occur. I'm not in charge. You are."

Lauren liked that idea. She felt she hadn't been in charge of anything in a long time. Bob and his wandering ways were a case in point.

"So, what happens next?"

"Well, let's start from the beginning."

After twenty minutes of explaining the process — confidentiality, length of engagement, the Coaching Binder containing tools and resources, and other details like Lauren's preference for visual learning, Andrea was direct. "What personally do you want to accomplish? What are your targeted outcomes?"

Lauren needed a minute to mull this over. Leaning back in her chair and gazing up at the white ceiling tiles, she realized she hadn't articulated such thoughts aloud to anyone. Her mind wandered to an office with windows and how much more pleasant it would be to stare out of them instead of at those ceiling tiles. Yet another reason to resent Peter Principle. Lauren chose to redirect the question away from herself.

"Have you ever worked with other institutional venture capitalists?"

"Yes. Several."

"Okay, then you're familiar with the intensity of a job like mine. I don't need coaching to set goals. I need more time in the day and more days in the week. Can you give me that?" Lauren tried to relax her body language and unfold her arms, knowing she was heating up. The amount of time in her workday required for coaching was making her angry and frustrated. And she knew her new coach was good, but she certainly was better. When it came to outsmarting others in meetings, she could run circles around her colleagues. This situation was no different.

The use of absolutes like "everything" is typically an indication of a blind spot.

"What are you *really* concerned about, Lauren?"

"Okay, Andrea. Honestly it just seems certain individuals get promoted for their relationships with the boss, regardless of their experience or track record, while others like me work hard and do *everything* but aren't appreciated."

Andrea let the words hang in the air. The silence invited Lauren to see her blind spots. The use of absolutes like "everything" is typically an indication of a blind spot.

In those few seconds, Lauren decided her opponent wasn't going to break easily. She needed a new strategy to put her in control of the conversation. Her day's workload loomed. "Look, this firm is complicated; my situation is complicated. I think I need to tell you my story of what's going on here and put it into context."

Lauren elaborated on the details about losing the promotion to Richard's college chum Peter, her tireless commitment to the firm, and her desperate need to keep her work and life in better balance. She went on about her dread of facing the other managers at the Tuesday board meeting. Everyone knew she lost her coveted position to Peter, and she was enormously embarrassed by the disdain or pity with which they'd likely view her.

Andrea listened intently, took some notes on questions Lauren had either long forgotten or never dared ask herself.

"What do you get for your perspective? Is there a payoff for you in having this perspective? What value does your perspective offer you?"

"Value? There's value in my perspective?"

Andrea nodded. "How can you describe your perspective?"

"Okay. Let's see. From my perspective: I'm right. They're wrong. And if I get to have others' pity and empathy I would consider that the payoff. But I don't really like how it feels to play victim." Lauren sipped her cold coffee with a feeling of self-loathing.

Kaizen, means "improve."

"That's what we're going to change. By little bits and pieces, five degrees at a time. It's like the Japanese method, *Kaizen*. Which means "improve." It's about taking small incremental steps to accomplish a goal. How can you look at this situation differently to get greater value? More significant value."

Reflection and Analysis Generate Small Steps, BIG Gains

A scotoma, or blind spot, happens when there's something we don't see about ourselves that others do see. This causes a block in understanding that prevents us from developing in a certain area and why feedback, mentoring and coaching are crucial to growth. We simply can't see ourselves completely without the support of others. The quote by Anaïs Nin, "We don't see things as they are, we see them as we are," is both enlightening and concerning. What if the way we are creates a cognitive dissonance, which results in us unintentionally ignoring a significant problem? What if our blind spot is the very thing blocking us from what we want? Then the way we are, the way we interpret our circumstances, needs to change. The Johari Window[4] offers an

"We don't see things as they are, we see them as we are." Anaïs Nin

---

[4] Johari Window is a technique created by Joseph Luft and Harry Ingham, 1955

illustration of the four quadrants. The top left quadrant is the part of ourselves we see and others see; the top right is the aspects others see of which we are unaware. Bottom right is the most mysterious part no one sees, and the bottom left is our private space, which we know but keep from others. We increase the size of the top left quadrant (open) in five degree increments by gaining relevant exposure and acquiring constructive feedback.

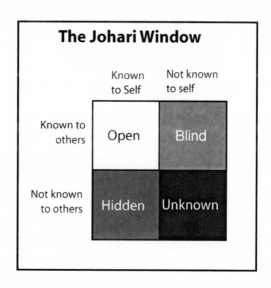

Create Your Own Five Degrees of Change

We all have blind spots. Those things about ourselves we either don't want to admit or truly don't see. Have the courage to consider what those could be for you. Your five degree shift may be to acknowledge that bad habit or tendency. Acknowledge it and know you have the power to eliminate it, minimize it, or keep doing it. If you keep doing it, recognize you can control it but choose not to.

Record your answers to these questions:

What potentially are your blind spots?

What feedback have you been given, directly or indirectly, that helps reveal something about yourself you may not know?

If your discovered blind spot is inconsistent with how you ideally want to be (i.e. you're impatient, you slurp your coffee, you say "I'm sorry" too much), what will you do to improve?

How will you evolve and develop in this area?

For help discovering your blind spot, consider these questions:

- **What bad habits do you relish** — and have you ever tried to give them up?
  - *Check email constantly, even at night and on vacation.*
  - *Assume negative intent.*
  - *Interrupt people.*
- **What chronic complaints do you have? (and how does your complaint impact your behavior?)**
  - *There's not enough time in the day.*
  - *My boss doesn't appreciate me.*
  - *No one works as hard as I do.*
- **What bad habits do you notice about other people? Are you ever guilty of those things?**
  - *Tardiness*
  - *Loud gum chewing*
  - *Talking with their mouth full*
  - *Self centered*
  - *Entitlement*

Keep Promises

"Action expresses priorities."

—Mahatma Gandhi
Leader of the Indian Nationalist Movement

It's easy to say you care about your kids, you want to be healthy, or you value peace and quiet. However, it's not always easy to support notions like these with your actions. Lauren recognizes her habit of choosing work over her kids. Even more than with her kids, her needs to be needed and feel important are met consistently at work. She's ashamed to admit she has a greater sense of worth and value from work, so she becomes addicted to it, yet struggles with the contradiction it presents to her core values. Lauren aspires to spend quality time with family to achieve an overall work/home/life balance. Her schedule and time, however, have not been in accordance with such great standards.

❖ ❖ ❖

As Lauren's coaching session ended, the light dawned on Lauren with this truth: work is a game. There are ways to gain points to improve your score, ways to lose points too. Lauren's fieldwork would include paying attention to the DEG game with a new lens of awareness.

As they were completing the meeting, Lauren's mind jumped from game playing, to a scoreboard, to a soccer field, to Daniel, to the science fair.

Who is winning at your work game?

"You're trained in managing complex issues and game playing, right? I've got a typically long, packed day today, you know — business-as-usual. But tonight my son has a science fair. Should I go?"

"I can identify with this type of tough decision, Lauren." Andrea described a hectic time in her career; her children were young, her husband had a demanding job and she was building her business. Her daughter had a Cherub Choir Christmas Concert and really wanted Andrea to attend. She had an important event in New York the day of the concert, asked her husband to videotape the performance, and assured her daughter she'd do her best to be there. Andrea left New York in time to make the show. But an unexpected snowstorm that night caused the trains to run late. The performance had begun while Andrea was still trying to get to her home train, and she ended up missing the entire show. She described seeing the videotape later, welling up with tears. The Cherub Choir was facing front to follow the lead of their music instructor. Daughter Tara's eyes were trained toward the entrance door of the church where Andrea would have come through. She wished she could have either declined the event, set different expectations with her daughter, or miraculously made it on time. Alas...

"Unfortunately I can't undo that night, Lauren. But maybe you can learn from it."

❖ ❖ ❖

After Andrea left, Lauren leafed through her sparse notes from their meeting. Though still skeptical about coaching, Lauren felt overwhelmed and had the nagging, fruitless feeling her career was stalling and heading down a dead-end street. It was beginning to dawn on her that perhaps help was needed to sort it all out. Lately her hypothetical questions to self about what she might do differently or how to change things surprisingly went unanswered. Lauren *always* had answers! If she asked herself a question before bedtime, generally she would awaken with at least a few options to pursue. *Worst-case scenario: coaching causes me to lose a few hours of my life. No worse than wasting a few hours at those awful company networking events.* Maybe Andrea could be that one person to shed some light on my issues and help me out of this mire. Right then and there, Lauren decided to try to embrace Richard's generous support.

She pondered her choices, her game-playing effectiveness and her future as she chewed her lip and tapped her pencil on the meeting notes. It occurred to her that the only time she gave thought to her future was on the fly while walking down the long corridor to her office. She smiled to herself. Mental note: Make *myself* a priority. *Schedule time for career and personal development.*

The phone rang as she was mulling this over. Lauren saw Suzie's name and picture pop up on the screen. "Hi, Suzie. Sorry I never got back to you."

"How *are* you?" Suzie's voice dripped with wanting to know all the painful details of recent events. "You must be devastated about this whole Peter thing. I mean, really, what was Richard thinking? What are ya gonna do? Tell Richard what he can do with his promotion? I don't know how you can stand it every day."

Schedule time for career and personal development.

Lauren was glad to hear a familiar voice but at the same time felt defensive. "Really, Suzie, it's bad, but it's not like I'm an indentured servant. I'm trying to figure things out. I'm just not there yet."

"You'd be a fool to stay. They don't appreciate you, and you'll never go anywhere at that company."

Lauren knew her friend meant well, but the negativity was grating on her. "Suzie — thanks for calling, but I have to run. Let's reconnect next week and schedule lunch, okay?"

Lauren hung up feeling guilty for cutting off her friend, but she needed a clear head, and listening to Suzie wasn't helping.

Am I a fool? That's it. She threw her pencil down on her desk. *I'm leaving at three to get to Daniel's science fair. I'm tired of feeling like I'm working hard and getting no respect or recognition.*

Daniel was thrilled to see her. The science fair was impressive and Daniel won an Innovation Award. *I almost missed this,* she thought, watching her son offer a firm handshake to the head of the Science Department, Mr. Michaels. He positively exuded confidence and made direct eye contact with Mr. Michaels and the teachers and students around him.

> **Be fully present with the kids. They deserve my attention.**

Atta boy. Lauren whispered to him proudly, under her breath. *Daniel's becoming a real gentleman!*

After sharing a celebratory dinner with the kids later that evening, Lauren nervously checked her email. Nothing major had happened after she left.

She questioned why she consistently chose work over her kids and why she was nervous to check her email. *I'm not that important!* She laughed to herself. A five degree change she could make occurred to her: *be fully present with the kids. They deserve my attention.*

Reflection and Analysis Generate Small Steps, BIG Gains

Actions speak louder than words. Not only did Lauren make Daniel a priority today, she realized there was no consequence to leaving work early. Sometimes we put so much unnecessary pressure focusing on the trees – being available, being involved, and being essential – we miss the forest. We miss the bigger picture: our life.

> **Keep your promises.**

"Little things" matter. Like setting appropriate expectations with your children, life partner or colleague. Say what you mean and mean with you say. Keep your promises – or don't make them.

Create Your Own Five Degrees of Change

- Clarify and manage your expectations with those close to you.
- Put yourself first (schedule time for something important to you, like time to think about your future).
- Tell someone you deeply care about that you love them, and why. Be present with them. The greatest gift you have to give is you.

> **The greatest gift you have to give is you.**

Additional Resources

Zeigler, K. Getting Organized at Work: 24 Lessons to Set Goals, Establish Priorities, and Manage Your Time. The McGraw-Hill Professional Education Series. 2005

Chandler, S. Time Warrior: How to defeat procrastination, people-pleasing, self-doubt, over-commitment, broken promises and chaos. Maurice Bassett. 2011

Richardson. C. Take Time for Your Life: A Personal Coach's 7-Step Program for Creating the Life You Want. Three Rivers Press. 1999.

Find Your Happiness and Success Formula

"Perhaps if one really knew when one was happy one would know the things that were necessary for one's life."

—Joanna Field
Author, A Life of One's Own

Would identifying the amount of time we allocate in our life's various areas – like work, family, fitness and the rest– help us figure out our individual happiness and success formula? What is the secret to happiness and success? In this chapter, Andrea helps Lauren identify and evaluate her level of fulfillment in the various elements of her life. Currently Lauren's formula has only two elements: work and kids. Lauren rediscovers how *variety* - the spice of life – is essential for personal fulfillment and happiness.

❖ ❖ ❖

The conference room smelled like stale coffee and leftover lunchmeat and cheese — the fast food of much of corporate America. The executive team's meeting ran an hour and fifty minutes longer than scheduled. Lauren was exhausted just from listening to all the positioning and posturing. She loathed the drama. Worse, the members were all so attached to their own agendas, nothing was actually getting accomplished.

"Clearly, we need more time to figure this out," Richard said, shuffling the reports into a neat stack. "We're going around in circles, and there are other things I need to get done today." He pushed his seat out from the head of the well-lacquered conference room table. It was clear the meeting was adjourned.

What is the secret to happiness and success?

Everyone looked around, afraid to disagree. Peter shrugged, Thomas nodded his head in agreement, Ray, another of Richard's "good ol' boys," cocked his head, and they all packed up their things. Lauren gathered up her folders and quickly followed Richard out of the room.

"Sometimes it's tough to get everyone's agreement," Lauren tried to console Richard.

"On anything, more like. Why can't people get things done around here? We have to complete the due diligence on these top companies so we know which ones we're investing in next year. Every second we waste, we lose money." Richard rolled his eyes and with frustration, exhaled loudly. "But I appreciate that you're always the peacemaker in there, Lauren. You don't cause trouble, and I really appreciate it."

Words convey meaning, intended or not.

What does THAT mean? Peacemaker? That's weak. I'm tough and can handle conflict! Before Lauren could question Richard about the meaning of his cryptic comment, her iPhone rang. It was already 4:25 and Andrea was probably waiting for her; after all, their appointment was 4:00.

"We'll get it done, Richard." Lauren offered an upbeat smile, consciously projecting an attitude of cooperation and confidence. "Gotta go meet Coach Lombardi." Lauren knew her attitude had been cold when Richard announced to her his "gift" of coaching. Wanting to make up for it, she tried for an air of enthusiasm. *Maybe I'm just masking my conflicted feelings.* The last thing she wanted to do was upset Richard. Lauren hated Richard to be angry with her, though she hated herself even more for caring.

"Glad you're making the most of coaching, Els. We're investing in you because you're worth it. Good ROI, you could say."

"Thanks, Richard," she said smiling genuinely.

Lauren walked briskly into her office, greeted Andrea, and dumped her files onto her already-overloaded desk. "How's your day going?" Andrea inquired.

"Hectic. Crazy! Busier than usual." The red blinking message light distracted Lauren, as did the full computer screen of new emails, overwhelming her with the sense that while the day was almost over, she needed time for Andrea and still needed to get home for the kids.

"What was your goal for the day?"

"Goal?"

"Yeah, what did you decide that your day should look like when you got up this morning?

"I just wanted to get through it," Lauren admitted. "My sitter just sent me a text telling me she's quitting her job with me…something about a boyfriend…so I called a neighbor to check on my kids after school — I got voicemail and left a message. They'll be home alone. Hope my neighbor gets the message. So, since you asked, dealing with the fall-out from my babysitter quitting wasn't what I'd intended as one of my goals today."

Andrea thought for a moment. "Lauren, as we discussed, if you're going to make changes in your life — and impact your career — they have to happen five degrees at a time, remember? You can't expect the one-eighty. So you must begin to think of the events in your life as 'five degree events' and manage them in small chunks."

Think of the events in your life as 'five degree events' and manage them in small chunks.

"What do you mean?"

"Well, your sitter quit. Was that event a life-changing event that will turn everything upside-down? Or was it a five degree event?"

"It feels pretty significant, but I see what you're saying. So I guess if I look at it in a smaller chunk like 'childcare,' I can find a simpler, five-degree method to deal with it?"

"Exactly, Lauren! Making change five degrees at a time is a key technique to achieve your ultimate goal. But you first have to *know* your goals and how they correlate to the vision you have for your life."

"If you had to identify what the number one thing is that you want to focus on now, what is it?" Andrea prepared to write.

"I want to get a grip on my career and my life."

"Okay, let's get a little more specific."

"Specifically?" Lauren squeezed her eyes shut while contemplating her specific goals.

"What I really want is to figure out the magic formula to how you grow your career *and* be an effective parent."

"Well, Lauren, there really is no one-size-fits-all formula. You have to figure out your own unique formula. Everyone does."

"That would be helpful. How do I start?" Lauren queried, hoping for clarity.

"Intangible goals like this are challenging to describe and measure.

Formula for Fulfillment. What are the areas in your life on which you want to focus?

Let's break down your life into the several important elements by creating your Formula for Fulfillment. Let's call it F2F."

Andrea drew a pie with eight slices. She put the number zero in the center and ten on the outermost part of each slice indicating the scale from not fulfilled (0) to fulfilled (10).

"What are the areas you want to focus on?"

"Let's see... Career, Kids, Fitness/Health, Community, Financial Well-being, Relationships/Friendships," Lauren thoughtfully stated possible elements.

Andrea labeled each pie slice with the categories Lauren identified.

"Two more. We need eight," Andrea encouraged as she filled in the labels for outer part of the circle.

"Guess I can break up the Relationships and Friendships," Lauren rolled her eyes reluctantly. "And, um, add in fun/recreation/hobbies."

"On a scale from zero to ten, how fulfilled are you in each area?"

"Zero in the fun/recreation category!"

Andrea made the notation.

"How should I measure my degree of fulfillment in each area? What will determine if I'm a ten, totally fulfilled – or void of this element – a big zero?"

"By assessing the amount of time, energy and focus you give to each area, combined with how satisfied you are."

"Like work – ten," Lauren quickly responded.

"Are you totally fulfilled at work?"

"No," Lauren said disappointedly. "I spend all my time here and am not totally fulfilled. Oooh, that's eye opening!" she winced.

"What number would you give it?"

"I'd give it an eight out of ten. My self-worth is wrapped up in my career right now." Seemingly ashamed, Lauren began to draw a pie chart with a **Are you totally fullfilled at work?** 90% slice and a 10% slice. She wrote "work" next to the largest piece and "the rest" next to the small one.

Working together with Andrea they went through each element of the wheel, giving them a rating from one to ten.

The completed chart looked like this:

"Okay," Andrea continued, "If this were an actual wheel, how would it feel…today?"

"It'd be a helluva ride!" Andrea and Lauren shared a much-needed laugh.

Andrea explained how the wheel created a snapshot of Lauren's current formula. "If you want *different* results, you'll need to tweak and shift each area until you come up with the right formula.

"Believe it or not, Lauren, the other elements *can* fit into your life. Five degrees at a time. Choose one element with a fulfillment rating much lower than you'd like. Commit to doing something to increase the rating."

If you want different results, you'll need to tweak and shift each area until you come up with the right formula.

"My role as a Mom. I want that to be a ten," Lauren said with a sense of hope and inspiration.

"What's one small thing you can do?"

"Get home to my kids – as soon as possible."

"Go for it, Lauren. We'll talk tomorrow." Andrea packed up her things, put the handwritten wheel on the Coaching Binder, touched Lauren lightly on the arm, and left.

This unplanned departure felt freeing! Lauren turned up the music on the car stereo and sang the whole way home. It felt good to be alive.

When she walked in the door, the kids were nowhere to be seen. She panicked, ran upstairs skipping every other step, and barged into Danny's room. Sure enough, he was engrossed in a video game.

"Mom, is that you?" Kelly called from her room.

"Yes, honey!" Lauren was breathless and incredulous as she crossed the threshold of Kelly's unusually tidy room. "What's this? It looks like a showroom."

"Funny, Mom. I just felt like cleaning up. Even *I* couldn't stand the junk everywhere."

"Well, that's something new! What brought this on?"

"Remember that new boy in class I told you about?"

"I sure do," Lauren responded softly.

"Mom, he likes me."

"So that's why you're cleaning your room?"

"Yeah, Mom. It's clean in case he decides to come over to see me."

Lauren's protective side stepped in. "Wait a minute! You're eleven. If you're going to entertain boys, it will be in the family room, and I'll be here when you do."

"Aw, Mom!"

"And, by the way, you'll be sixteen before that even happens."

"Mom!"

"Don't 'Mom' me, Kelly. I am surprised you think he'd be allowed over."

Kelly looked up with anger, "You don't get it, Mom. He likes me!"

Lauren knew Kelly was experiencing attraction for perhaps the first time. She had to step out of guardian role and try to understand her daughter. Lauren gave Kelly a big hug.

"Of course I get it, Kelly. There's a *lot* to like about you! He's a wise young man. Guess there are several little changes happening for us. You becoming more interested in boys is one. We're making changes, five degrees at a time, honey. That means you're free to text him and talk on the phone. No visits however. Not yet."

In that instant, Lauren finally realized the consequences of both not changing and making sudden, one-eighty turns. Turn five degrees at a time, and your transition — your turn — is likely to be pretty smooth.

In the midst of this meaningful moment with her daughter, she thought to herself, I'm going to help Kelly — and Danny, too — make five degree changes.

"How about you, Mom? How are the five degree changes working for you? Is your boss starting to like you too?" Lauren had to laugh at thoughts of Richard being amiable towards her outside of the usual boss-underling relationship.

"I think so, Kelly. I really think so. I can tell he has a good heart." She kissed Kelly and said, "Come into my room, I want to talk with you and your brother."

Daniel put down the video controller and followed Kelly to Lauren's room. She patted the bed to invite them to sit down next to her. They seemed nervous, like she was about to share bad news.

"I want to be a better Mom," she began, "and I need some advice on what I need to do more or less to be better."

"You're a good Mom already," Daniel offered sincerely.

Kelly distractedly began fluffing a pillow. "Yeah, Mom, we know you work hard."

"Thank you for your kind words. I want to be better. Tell me one thing, one small thing I can do to be better. Please."

Daniel suggested Lauren have more fun with them. He said she always reminds them about rules and routines and needs more play time.

Tell me one thing, one small thing, I can do to be better.

Kelly expressed her desire to have more time to talk. She was thankful Lauren was home early tonight.

Lauren kissed her children lovingly and initiated a group hug. They laughed and agreed to have fun competing on one of the video games. Playfully following the kids to Daniel's room, Lauren smiled as an old adage came into her mind: "When the student is ready, the teacher appears."

Reflection and Analysis Generate Small Steps, BIG Gains

Taking a close look at all the areas of our lives helps us identify which get most of our focus and energy and which get least. Once we outline those areas, we can try to balance our priorities. Happiness comes from being specific about what you want and allocating the right amount of time to get it. The result is our own unique success formula. Lauren knew she'd over-indexed her focus on career but didn't realize there were so many other pieces of life to consider! Taking one step at a time, she can reallocate her time and figure out her unique success formula.

Create Your Own Five Degrees of Change

Complete your own Formula for Fulfillment. The eight sections in the Formula for Fulfillment represent harmony in the segments of life most relevant to you. Seeing the center of the wheel as zero and the outer edge as ten, rank your level of satisfaction with each life area by drawing a curved line to create a new outer edge. The new perimeter of the circle represents the Formula for Fulfillment. How bumpy would the ride be if this were a real wheel?

Additional Resources

Avigdor, B. and Greenberg, C. What Happy Working Mothers Know: How New Findings in Positive Psychology Can Lead to a Healthy and Happy Work/Life Balance. Kindle Edition. 2009.

Merrill, A.R. Life Matters: Creating a dynamic balance of work, family, time, and money. McGraw-Hill. 2004.

Improve the Quality of Your Questions

"We thought that we had the answers,
it was the questions we had wrong."

—Bono

Musician and Humanitarian

One of the lies of leadership is, as leaders, we must know all the answers. That simply isn't possible or even true. The secret to effective leadership is *knowing the right questions to ask*. Thought-provoking, open-ended and strong questions will encourage others to think more creatively and strategically. The questions you ask put you either on a road of darkness or a road of possibility. Which road you choose determines how much progress and satisfaction you can achieve.

In Chapter Nine, Lauren learns about how the questions she asks herself can exert a powerful, and not always positive influence on her results and choices. Her coach shares a practical tool with her to help her stay on the right road.

◆ ◆ ◆

Lauren thought about her goals and the Formula for Fulfillment on her drive home. She thought about them when she awakened in the morning, in every meeting, at lunchtime, and when she went to bed. She kept asking herself, "Why haven't I thought about these things before?"

Andrea arrived promptly for their 4:00 pm meeting. Lauren was glad they were meeting more frequently. She appreciated Andrea's support, trusted her, and no longer felt wary of the coaching process. She sensed herself gaining momentum and clarity.

"Did you give some thought to your goals last night?"

"Funny you should ask. I couldn't *stop* thinking about them."

"What conclusions did you reach?"

One of the lies of leadership is, as leaders, we must know all the answers.

Lauren shrugged and shook her head. "First, I can't stop thinking about why I never really thought about my goals before. Typically, I would work hard and hope things just work out. Last night my goal was to boost my low scores in the "fun" and "kids" elements of my life, so I just focused on having a good time with them. As for my career – our primary coaching focus – I journaled about my number one goal. It is to be Venture Partner in this firm. But I can't help feeling the deck is stacked against me."

"So you resent that?"

"Totally. I keep asking myself, *"Why didn't they promote me?"*"

"Lauren, you just asked yourself a very revealing question."

"I did?"

"Yes, absolutely."

"Let's step back before we step forward," Andrea continued. "Most of our thoughts are in the form of questions. Think about this morning. It started with your alarm. You probably asked a string of questions like:

'What time is it?'

'Why don't I get enough sleep?'

'How long can I snooze?'

'Should I work out today?'

'Should I get some extra sleep and run at lunch?'

'Should I work out after work or maybe even tomorrow?'

'What's the weather?'

'What should I wear today?'

'What do I have going on today?'

'Do I have an event tonight?'

"And on and on from there. All those questions — and that's only the FIRST thirty seconds of your day! Am I right?'"

"Yes! Were you there?" Lauren laughed. "But you missed one. 'Why didn't I get the promotion?' I ask that one every day when I'm getting ready."

"Lauren, that's your **chronic** question. The queen mother of all your questions." Andrea explained how the majority of our thoughts are in the form of a question. If we understand the power of questions, the quickest route to improving the quality of our lives is to improve the quality of our questions!

"Beware of the chronic questions. The lead questions. They influence *all* the others, control you, and rob you of the energy and strength you need to locate practical solutions." With her tone of voice and intense look into Lauren's hazel eyes, Andrea tried to transmit to Lauren the need to exercise caution when asking herself those potent questions that can result in travelling the wrong road. She handed Lauren a picture. "Here's a graphic map of the sorts of choices we all make. Put it someplace where you see it every day."

Lauren studied the full-color image for a moment and had a powerful *aha!* moment. "I think this is telling me I'm asking the wrong questions."

Andrea didn't respond to Lauren's statement directly. Instead, she said, "The questions you ask are always aligned with your focus. We get what we focus on — positive or negative. There are only two types of questions: Disempowering and Empowering."

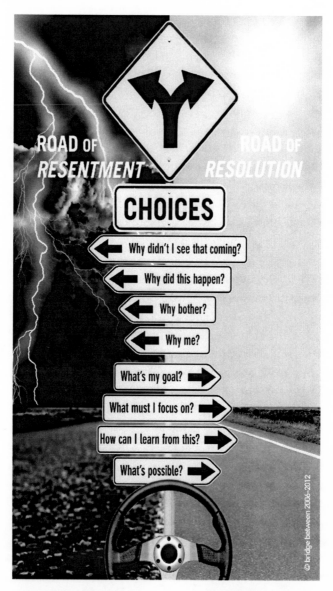

DISEMPOWERING:
Focuses on the problem
Leaves you stuck
You're a victim

EMPOWERING:
Focuses on solutions
Moves you to action
Gives you the control

"Check out the road of resentment to the left. It's dark and gray. Questions on the road of resentment are accusatory and negative interrogatories: 'Why did I do that?', 'Why me?', 'Why bother?'

"While you're walking on the road of resentment, you might be feeling hopeless, helpless, pessimistic, negative, depleted, depressed, or uptight.

"On the other side is the Road of Resolution! It's bright; the sun is shining. It's a road of inquiry and possibility."

Lauren smiled and nodded in agreement. "Quite a difference!"

"Questions you might ask on the road of resolution include: 'How can I be a leader in this situation?', 'What can I learn from this?', 'How can I continue to add value?' 'How can I stay essential?' You may feel lighter, upbeat, curious, optimistic, or empowered when you walk here."

Lauren nodded. "I can see how my choice of road affects me and those around me. I can physically feel the difference when I ask myself those questions."

Andrea was reminded of the C.S. Lewis quote,

"We all want progress, but if you're on the wrong road, progress means doing an about-turn and walking back to the right road; in that case, the man who turns back soonest is the most progressive."
—*C. S. Lewis*

Andrea gave Lauren a new assignment. "In the coming days, be acutely aware of which road you take. Notice when you're in darkness. Ask a better question. Bounce back. SNAP! Be resilient. Feel empowered to choose a different road." Andrea explained how we author the questions we ask and can rewrite disempowering questions to create stronger possibilities. Just before Andrea left Lauren's office she made one more request. "While you're at it, rewrite *'Why didn't I get promoted?'* and see if it makes a difference."

Ask a better question. Bounce back. SNAP! Be resilient.

Lauren thought about her questions. Do I think in questions? She laughed inwardly, realizing *that* was a question. That evening she shared what she learned with the kids, and they attached the visual to the fridge to remind themselves to stay on the Sunny Side, as they referred to it.

Attempting to apply the concept to problem-solving, Daniel said, "I think my chromrick question is *why do I have to do homework.*" "Chronic, Daniel. It means continuing all the time, a question that keeps coming into your head. Like a habit. What's a better question to ask?"

"How can homework help me?"

"Awesome, Daniel. Nice job," Lauren was pleased to see the kids also learning from her new tools and insights.

After putting the kids to bed, Lauren reached over to grab the journal, the dust mark suddenly filling her vision. *Why can't this house ever be clean?* This time she caught her Road of Resentment question and, SNAP! She changed direction. *How can I appreciate this house?* She felt better already.

Chronic questions I ask every day: Why do I have to do all of this on my own (clean, cook, homework with kids, fix things in the house, mow lawn, shop for kids and me, banking, lunches, driving kids to sports and friends…) and my work (planning, selling, email, meetings, managing my career, managing my team, managing my supervisors?

New questions: How can I get more energy to meet the demands of my life? Or, what am I grateful for? That will help me keep things in perspective. I'm so blessed to have a job and healthy children. I need to remember to be more thankful. New chronic question: How can I be even more grateful for this moment, now?

Okay, and lately my question is, why didn't I get promoted? That's a tough one. How about: How can I be the absolute best in my role? What can I focus on that will make me indispensable? How can I over-deliver on my goals and still have life balance?

Oooh, these are good.

Lauren pulled out her phone and texted these questions to herself, aware she was in the process of building a new habit to alter negative perspectives and build more positive ones. Texting herself seemed like just the reminder that would work best in the learning-to-establish-a-new-habit game.

Reflection and Analysis Generate Small Steps, BIG Gains

If the majority of your thoughts are in the form of a question, the quickest way to improve the quality of your life is to improve the quality of your questions. Until today, Lauren believed she needed to know all of the answers. Her self-worth was a derivative of her intellectual contribution and subject matter expertise. She was unaware of the power of asking questions — to herself or to others.

> **If the majority of your thoughts are in the form of a question, the quickest way to improve the quality of your life is to improve the quality of your questions.**

Create Your Own Five Degrees of Change

Something as small as a question can change your life. Albert Einstein said, "If I had an hour to solve a problem and my life depended on the solution, I would spend the first 55 minutes determining the proper question to ask, for once I know the proper question, I could solve the problem in less than five minutes."

When you catch yourself heading down the Road of Resentment (note: you know you're there if you feel irritated, stressed, negative, drained, etc.), stop, SNAP! Go back and plant your feet — and your mind — on the Road of Resolution (how you feel on this path: light, joyful, energized, positive, happy).

Questions are a source of life change and a fundamental key to success. Intentionally asking the right questions is a way to play an entirely different game. Empowering questions tend to start with What or How. *What is your new empowering question?*

Additional Resources

Leeds, D. The 7 Powers of Questions: Secrets to Successful Communication in Life and at Work. Perigee Trade. 2000

Barker, R. The Power of Decision. Tarcher, 2011.

Adams, M. Change Your Questions, Change Your Life: 10 Powerful Tools for Life and Work. Berrett-Koehler. 2009

Make-A-DecisionPad by Knock Knock. amazon.com/makea decisionnotepad

Create New Possibilities

> *"The happiness of your life
> depends on the quality of your thoughts."*
>
> —Marcus Aurelius Antoninus
> *Roman Emperor and Philosopher*

A lever is a small object that dramatically improves our ability to move something heavy. We use personal levers to get ourselves to do something we don't really want to do.

The Ladder of Leverage coaching tool introduced in this chapter is designed to help us recognize we have power and control. It's yet another way to look at free will, perception, and choice. Lauren needs to exert greater control and exhibit more power in order to grow. She's learning how to be the CEO of her career and has some new choices to make.

❖ ❖ ❖

It had been another hectic day, starting with the kids' ride to school falling through, making her just late enough to irritate Richard. He made sure to let Lauren know he was annoyed. Lauren's timing, responsiveness and energy were off the entire day. She joined the meeting unprepared, lost the dial-in number for a client conference call, re-read emails several times without getting a handle on them, and forgot to bring her water bottle with her the three times she went to fill it up.

Lauren was introspective as she hit the break room coffee machine. She didn't notice her trusted colleague Sohan staring over her shoulder.

"You really need to switch to green tea." Sohan, stood behind her with a broad grin on his face.

"Hey, there. You still trying to convert me? You know I can't live without my coffee."

"Yes, I know, but I'm going to keep trying until you listen. If you took better care of yourself, you'd feel better." Sohan's meditative voice teased her with a promise of better job performance through healthy living. He knew Lauren was only interested in solutions with tangible outcomes. He handed her an herbal tea bag that looked like potpourri. "Promise me you will brew this and drink it today."

"Or put it in my drawer for fragrance. That's too pretty to boil."

"Promise?"

When life boils your kettle, make tea!

"Okay. I promise. *When life boils your kettle, make tea!*" She enjoyed a good laugh with Sohan while quoting from friend Michele's email signature. Uplifted by the exchange, Lauren headed to her office with a renewed desire to embrace change in her work attitude.

Lauren tried to focus on finishing an overview of her recent challenges and outline them in bullet points, aware she was slipping behind in her work. She wondered if her time would be better spent catching up than completing her coaching assignments. Just as she was grappling with her ambivalence, she heard Andrea in the hall approaching her door. After their usual exchange of pleasantries, Lauren's words exposed a defeatist attitude and feelings about things being worse than ever.

"I just can't get it right."

"Lauren, I think there's something going on in your mind — in your life — that you can't see."

"Okay…I'll bite. What's that?"

"You have 'limiting beliefs.' These are the things that stop you from moving ahead."

"Um…okay. What are they?" Lauren felt defensive.

"Well, let's begin with what you've told me your beliefs are about Richard and DEG."

This big subject provided Lauren the perfect motivating question to ask herself. She let a vision of Richard and company dynamics fully enter her consciousness, the imagery of which was rife with feelings of marginalization and exclusion. She could feel her negativity build while envisioning the partners gathered behind closed doors laughing and chumming it up, and Richard's reaction to her when she was late for the meeting that had never previously started on time.

"Give me an example of a limiting belief you have. Something you can't control that gets in your way."

"How about this: I'm not political enough. I don't want to play the dirty corporate politics game; I won't get ahead."

"Let's focus on the belief that corporate politics is dirty." Andrea began to draw an oval and the image of a ladder coming up from the oval on Lauren's dry-erase board. In the oval she wrote, "stuff."

"So many things happen in any given day — conversations, assignments, messages, challenges, projects, wins, losses, etc. Let's call that 'stuff that happens.' " The black marker squeaked as Andrea began to fill in the steps.

"Because all this stuff puts so many demands on our attention, we sift through the input and data and pick only **some** of the stuff on which to focus, and delete the rest.

"Those selections have value and meaning. They're interpreted as the **truth**. We believe the meaning we've given to our selected stuff *is a* **fact**. From that place, we create stories. We begin to tell a **story** about the stuff so it makes sense to others and us – a story we accept as "the truth." Basically we're all searching for meaning and a way to understand our stuff."

Stuff

"I'm following you, I think." Lauren nodded. "We do this probably without challenging our beliefs or story."

"Exactly. We establish 'beliefs' through making our interpretation of our stuff. We make that stuff into stories, and those stories become our beliefs."

If I'm the author of my story, I surely have written a doozie. I choose? I really have an option of which "stuff" I choose? I could consider all of what's happened as curves on the road rather than dead-ends. Interesting.

"Then we make choices from the stuff we chose, now in the form of stories. What choices are you making from the 'stuff' on which you chose to focus, and what story have you told about it?"

In being honest with herself, Lauren realized she chose to select elements from her Career Stuff associated with failure, frustration and fear, unwittingly deleting the moments of success and positive impact. Instead of focusing on the list of prospective DEG investments she proposed last year — companies that went public at 20 times their earnings, generating a recorded return of five times DEG's original investment – she focused on the email she accidentally sent to the wrong person or the typo on the PowerPoint presentation.

Lauren realized she needed to go back down the ladder to reselect and rewrite the stories she'd been telling herself and others.

She chose to select and focus on different stuff, like the positive financial contribution she'd made to the firm. DEG's ROI on her, as Richard often would tout.

> **Go back down the ladder to reselect and rewrite the stories.**

The truthful story she now authored is: *I am a valuable asset to this firm and a trusted member of the team. I'm as equal as I believe I am. Now that's a new story! With that interpretation, my beliefs empower me to truly get it this time and start focusing on what is working instead of what isn't.*

◆ ◆ ◆

Before bed that night, Lauren wrote some thoughts about the day.

Epiphany of the day: Choice. I never understood the incredible liberty of choice. I thought "stuff happens" and you deal with it. Today I learned to broaden my awareness of the stuff and choose what to focus on.

Most of my choices are not deliberate and intentional. They just capture how I'm thinking at the moment, I guess. From my "stuff" pool, I often choose things that are painful: money issues, challenges with Richard, kid stuff, not enough time, in my forties and alone. If I go back down the ladder and choose new stuff — what else is there?

So if it's about "possibility," that means no limits, right? Okay, then this is what's in my pool of choices: other careers with less stress and higher compensation, appreciation for Richard (he means well), all the things I love about Kelly and Daniel (so many). I have more than enough time for the things that matter most. Including a relationship. Maybe it's time I start to open up to having another relationship. Bob found someone. He's happy. One thing at a time. Let's stay focused on work for now.

She smiled at her self-awareness and thought, *small changes make sense.*

Reflection and Analysis Generate
Small Steps, BIG Gains

"Stuff selection" is serious business and often happens automatically, without conscious awareness. Choosing poisonous stuff creates a nightmare story – a toxic truth, likely leading to an undesirable future. Lauren begins to taste real empowerment. Permission to rewrite her stories will offer her freedom to design her future. Her openness to considering new possibilities about her career and personal life will certainly change the course she's taking, and ultimately, her final destination. The small changes add up quickly when they involve reselecting "stuff" to create empowering beliefs for a new future.

Create Your Own Five Degrees of Change

All positive and limiting beliefs begin with "stuff" like information, experiences, conversations, and situations. From all of the thousands of semantic, emotional, and psychological meanings underlying the stuff, we select a handful of pieces and delete the rest. We tell ourselves what we've selected is real, the truth — a fact. From that position, we create stories. We add meaning, color, and context, either real or perceived. The meaning we create becomes a belief that we adamantly believe, defend, and attempt to prove.

From that same fictitious personal creation – entirely made up by and for ourselves, we create our future. The choices we make are built upon these stories we have written for ourselves. If you have a habit, belief, or negative tendency, walk back down the ladder, choose different stuff and *create a new possibility*.

- Think about why you do certain things and avoid others.
- Pick one thing, belief or habit you want to change.
- Walk down the Ladder of Leverage.
- Look at your selection of facts/data/circumstances/"stuff" and select something new.
- How does choosing that, over what you left behind, enable you to tell a different story?

- What's your goal? Does your new choice help you achieve your goal? If not, go back down and try again.
- Take responsibility for your choices.
- Dream about your future.

Ladder of Leverage[5]

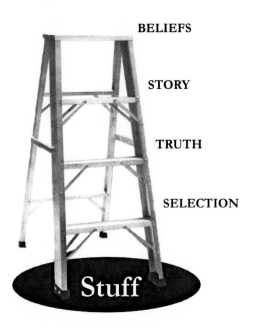

BELIEFS

STORY

TRUTH

SELECTION

Stuff

Additional Resources

Senge, P. The Fifth Discipline: The Art & Practice of The Learning Organization.

Frankl, V . Man's Search for Meaning. Beacon Press. 2006.

Dyer, W. Excuses Begone!: How to Change Lifelong, Self-Defeating Thinking Habits. Hay House. 2011.

---

[5]Adapted from The Ladder of Inference model from Harvard Business professor Chris Argyris and book The Fifth Discipline: The Art and Practice of The Learning Organization by Peter M. Senge

Rewrite Your Limiting Stories

"We are the stories we tell ourselves."

—Shekhar Kapur
Filmmaker

Each rung on the ladder in Chapter Eleven is critical to any significant change. When something happens and we add language to describe it, we create meaning. The meanings we create become our stories - the stories of our lives. Lauren is guilty of creating disempowering meaning, beliefs, and stories. Her stories are so real, they're controlling her. In this chapter, Lauren learns how to rewrite those stories to create and encourage new meaning for her life.

❖ ❖ ❖

Lauren handed Andrea a bottle of water and slid into the comfortable, overstuffed leather chair in the corner of her office.

"I have good news and bad news." Lauren tried to open this session on her own terms, and with humor. "The good news is that I didn't tell Richard to go to hell yesterday when I should have."

"Well done, I think…" Andrea laughed hesitantly.

"The bad news is, I'm still hung up on Peter. It feels like a force beyond my control!" Lauren's mind flashed through her bills, Richard, Bob, stress, fatigue. Her neck and shoulders began to burn as she felt her tension mount. It seems as if the pool of stuff at the foot of the ladder is shark water. *One minute I'm on top of the world, full of possibility and hope. The next, I'm down in the pit again. Having a tough time staying on the Sunny Side.*

> **We can sometimes become addicted to our problems.**

Andrea explained that building a fortress on the Sunny Side (Road of Resolution) while mocking the fools who go to the dark side (Road of Resentment) is the wrong way to go. Daily, hourly – whenever – we all go to the dark side. When unexpected inconveniences happen, we tend to go negative. The trick is to recognize you're on the dark side, ask a better question and snap back. When you find yourself drowning in the shark pool, grab hold of a life saver – a better question – and save yourself.

"What's a better question, Lauren?"

The concept of rewriting one's stories intrigued Lauren. "How can I tell a better story?"

Pleased to hear Lauren try to ask herself an empowering question, Andrea quickly recalibrated to illustrate the concept of storytelling from a new angle. The tool Lauren decided to use might make more sense and be helpful for those times in the future when she felt as if she were stuck. "Good. Let's dissect the event of Peter's promotion,

> **What does *that* story mean to you?**

which seems to underlie a lot of your current career unhappiness. What does *that* story mean to you?"

"I'll – I'll tell you what it means. The guy took my job! It means they're more interested in promoting fraternity friends and keeping the good ol' boy network alive than in making good decisions for this firm. It means they don't stand by the company values of 'diversity, respect and integrity' on the DEG website."

"What specifically seems like a lack of diversity, respect and integrity to you?" Andrea was beginning to draw a grid on her notepad.

"Well for starters, they clearly don't value diversity. The fact that I'm a woman and don't have the same college alumni association with whom to network is a disadvantage for me. I've worked hard. I'm the hardest working member of this team. I paid my dues and did my time. And integrity? *Please.* I'm the only one who doesn't regularly throw teammates under the bus. Peter would sell out his own mother if he thought it would get him ahead."

Andrea nodded to let Lauren know she was hearing her vent, while her grid took shape. Entitled, "Your Story," it had four columns, headed, left to right, 'X, The Facts';'Your Lead Story'; 'What Does That Mean About You'; and finally 'Three Alternative Stories.'

"Remember last week when we spoke about questions and meaning, stories, and the Ladder of Leverage?" Lauren nodded into her coffee, recognizing she often walked on the road of darkness.

"You said you like visual learning. Here's another fancy drawing for a new framework we can use. It's from Dr. Sharon Melnick's work and book *Success Under Stress.* The model breaks down what we've been working on another way. What are the facts? Peter got promoted, right?" As she answered her own question, Andrea began to write **Peter got promoted** in the grid's first column.

"What have you made that *mean?* Once you add words to facts, you create meaning. What does this fact mean to you?"

"Fraternity, ol' boy network, Ivy League, blah, blah, blah. Is that what you mean by 'what have I made it mean?' "

"Yes, exactly. Your lead story, including language choices like *'the guy who took my job,'* is your current way of explaining what happened. And it's not serving you. In this story, you're powerless. It's them against you. You're the victim. What does **that** lead story, **that** interpretation, say about **you?**"

Andrea looked at Lauren almost apologetically. She put her pen down and waited for an honest response. Lauren paused to think about how she'd given up her power to choose. *I've thought of myself as a victim. I've behaved like a child who hasn't gotten what I want. I'm embarrassed we've spent so much time on this one issue. Why can't I get past it? My sour grapes attitude must be showing everywhere.*

"It means I'm a sore loser and that maybe I'm afraid my career is going nowhere? Or that I'm bitter, or angry, or insecure." Lauren hoped she was on the right track in following her coach's direction.

Andrea wanted Lauren to find the answer for herself. "Only you know what it means, Lauren. What does it mean about *you*?" she prompted.

"It means I've worked my whole life to be the best, the smartest, the most successful. I want to make a difference in this company, in the world. I have big goals, and I don't want some BS political game to screw me out of what I offer."

Wavering between anger and relief, Lauren paused. *What is my problem? Why can't I get beyond this? I'm wasting so much time going over and over the same crap! I want to know my own worth and show up as confident and positive. I've got to take these tools and really* try *them. Not just 'get it' and divert back to this negative space.*

Then she inhaled slowly. *I refuse to stay stuck. I'm standing dead set in my way. Andrea must be so sick of my inability to get this stuff. Push yourself, Lauren, step up, be brave. Really get it this time. Come on.*

Big exhale. "What does 'my story' say about me? It says I'm still angry, resentful, and uncertain about my future."

"Does this recent setback to your plans mean you've changed your goals?" Andrea asked.

"Sure. I mean, I guess." Lauren looked down, distractedly, writing some notes.

"Do you still feel you need to reach a goal of becoming Venture Partner to make a difference in the world?"

"No," Lauren admitted sheepishly. *It's true — no, I don't. Nonetheless, it means a lot to me to move higher in the ranks where I feel I can do the most good.*

At this moment, Andrea shared an insight about identity. She said the strongest force in human nature is self identity. The most powerful driver of our behavior is the need to be consistent with how we see ourselves. If you see yourself as a victim, you are a victim. If you see yourself as a leader, you are a leader. Andrea encouraged Lauren to take responsibility for her self identity and how it shapes her. Then she offered another tool to help her visualize it. One thing you can do is design stories and create meanings that empower you. Give me three alternative interpretations of 'the facts' as you see them." Pen in hand, Andrea prepared to write.

Lauren tried identifying herself as a leader, rallied her intellect for creative genius. "Three alternatives? Well…one, they're testing me to see if I've got what it takes. Two, this is not a good place for me to work, and this situation is an indication that I need to make a change." Lauren's posture began, barely perceptibly, to change. She slouched down a bit lower in her chair. Leaving DEG was an option she'd contemplated, but dreaded facing. "Three, this is an opportunity to adapt and manage like an effective and influential leader."

You're the author of your story.

"The truth is," Andrea said calmly, "your first alternative is possible but could result in your feeling anxious and paranoid. Your second represents a really big change you might not feel ready to encompass. The third, a really good, five degree alternative, is one you might find most effective. Remember, you're the author of your story, Lauren."

Lauren understood how authoring and recording her own stories — if necessary, new stories — could enable her to create an interpretation consistent with her focus and goal. She needed to think carefully about her alternatives, realizing how powerful indeed those thoughts could be in shaping end results. It's all about choosing the direction most likely to get to that goal/get results. She knew her last alternative was how she wished her story to end, but how was she going to go about making that new story a reality? Suddenly she broke into a slow, "I got it" smile. Lauren *was* getting it, ever since Andrea queried her about whether her goal of becoming Venture Partner was key to her making a difference in the world. Added to the notion of adapting and managing like an effective influential leader, a thought blossomed: *While I really would* like *to be Venture Partner, maybe there's another way I can add great value to the firm. Do something new and fresh that I'm excited about! Maybe I could create a new path for DEG and me? This would be a five degree change from where I am currently, and I don't have to do a 180 – like leave DEG.*

Reflection and Analysis Generate
Small Steps, BIG Gains

If we could peel back the layers of our behaviors and beliefs, we could see the original facts of what happened and how we make our circumstances our stories. We attach language and meaning to them and think they're real. Lauren's awareness of her choices and authorship are becoming clear, and she is inspired to create new meaning in her life. She must rewrite the fundamentals of her story to interpret the facts differently. She can't just put icing over her problem and pretend it's a cake, like it's not there. She needs to reframe the facts to create a new possibility. If she improves her self identity and rewrites her story, she can be the victor.

We can't put icing over our problems and pretend they are a cake.

Create your own Five Degrees of Change

Here's a clean version of the chart Andrea drew for Lauren. Take a conflict in your life, an incident that bothers you and nags at your psyche. Complete the chart and see how you can change YOUR story!

Think of an event or situation that resulted in you feeling mad, angry, upset, stressed, etc. Ask these questions while you complete the chart. Write your own story. Create your conclusions.

- List only the facts of what happened.
- Bullet point what you made those events, things, and people mean. What is your lead story?
- What does that story say about you? What can you learn about yourself from the story you're telling about what happened?
- What else could it mean? Be creative, outrageous, and innovative. Come up with three alternative meanings.
- Choose the meaning that best serves you and your goals.

"X" Happens (facts)	Lead Story (what you make it mean)	What does that mean about you?	Three Alternative Stories

© Adapted from Sharon Melnick, Ph.D., Author of Success Under Stress, www.sharonmelnick.com

Additional Resources

Loehr, J. E. The Power of Story: Change Your Story, Change Your Destiny in Business and in Life. Free Press. 2008.

Baldwin, C. Storycatcher: Making Sense of Our Lives through the Power and Practice of Story. New World Library. 2007

Simmons, A. Whoever Tells the Best Story Wins: How to Use Your Own Stories to Communicate with Power and Impact. AMACOM. 2007

Choose Connections
Carefully

*"Don't be trapped by dogma – which is living with the results
of other people's thinking. Don't let the noise of other's
opinions drown out your own inner voice. And most important,
have the courage to follow your heart and intuition.*

—Steve Jobs
American Entrepreneur and Apple Computer Co-Founder

In order to evolve, Lauren needs all the energy, support and focus
she can get. She must surround herself with positive reminders,
courageous friends, and encouraging coaches who will help her stay
above the fray. She must guard herself against negativity, pessimism,
and scarcity thinking. Sometimes friends' own personal limiting
beliefs and disempowered stories distract us from the goals we've
established, and are unsafe for us. She must follow her heart and
intuition and listen to her inner voice.

❖ ❖ ❖

Lauren's day was intense. It was late afternoon; she looked
through the breakroom window at ominous skies, having that
old familiar feeling of wishing she could just head home now and

spend a quiet night with Kelly and Danny. *They really need me now—more than ever.*

She'd hit the wall at just about 5:00 and felt she needed a cup of coffee to get through the final hours. As if on auto pilot she walked to her office, dug into her drawer and pulled out the pretty potpourri tea bag Sohan gave her. *I'll make tea instead.* She smiled to herself about making a five degree shift in beverage choice. The day had been long and the night promised to be even longer. There were two reports on her desk to edit and complete, and she still needed to return three calls to clients on the West Coast.

Have the courage to follow your heart and intuition.

The last Friday night of the month was also happy hour. At the end of the month, Richard liked to watch his team bond at Buckley's, the Irish pub in the bottom floor of their building. Though the evenings could be fun, they tended to go on longer than Lauren wished. And she always hated to be viewed as the first one leaving. She suspected her co-workers assumed she was rushing home to play mommy to her kids. Truth be told, she often preferred her children's company to that of her co-workers with whom she spent 10, sometimes 12 hours a day. Still, there **were** times it was fun to vent, laugh, and unwind.

Richard started to make the rounds promptly at 6:00 p.m., stopping at each manager's office, reminding them to head down. Richard poked his head in Lauren's door. "Hey Els — first round's on me. Rally the troops, and let's get going! The beer's not getting any colder." Richard slapped the doorframe twice to emphasize urgency. Same line every month, and every month Richard laughed at himself.

She muted the phone call she was on to respond, "Yup, I'm coming in just a minute."

"There's nothing on your desk that can't wait until Monday! Ha ha." Richard moved to the next office door. He meant well, but would be the first to ask Monday morning at 8:00 why her reports weren't finished. In that instant Lauren intuitively decided to write her own story. She was not going to perceive Richard as micro-managing her; it was her choice to get the work done so she could enjoy her weekend. Her actions were not going to arise out of Richard's wants and needs. She followed her heart and decided what **she** wanted was to spend 45 minutes getting the two reports filed, then head down for Richard's reindeer games. She viewed happy hour a reward for hard work. Every once in a while it was fun to hang out with the guys.

> **Socializing with coworkers builds stronger relationships.**

Just as she was finishing with the work due Monday morning, Lauren's iPhone rang and she looked down to see Suzie's name. "Hey Suzie," she answered wearily. "What's up?"

"Tired and grateful it's Friday. What's up with you? Have you shot Richard yet?"

"Stop. Be nice. You know, Suzie, I'm trying really hard. This coaching thing has been an eye-opener — I'm starting to feel like me again — the 'me' who was always calling the shots, in control of her career. I felt like I was in a tailspin for so long, I forgot it was **my** hand on the wheel all the time—not Richard's. I'm good now and I think I can make it work here at DEG."

"*Really*? Richard will never promote you, you'll never move forward, and you'll always be unhappy there. I've told you a million times, you need to quit your job before it kills you."

"That's just the thing, Suz. There will always be a Richard and office politics. It's not about others. It's about me, and *me* is the part I'm changing. **And** I'm doing it *exactly* as my coach advises — five degrees at a time."

"If you say so. But I still think it's a losing proposition. Give me a call sometime this weekend," Suzie offered.

"This weekend is packed. Gotta run. Take good care, Suzie." Lauren hung up. She was not about to let anyone sabotage her career. *It's time to pull back from Suzie and surround myself with some positive energy.* Lauren packed up her laptop, rode the elevator and had a laugh with Allan and Mark, and headed to Buckley's.

The team had begun to gather on the far side of the long granite bar and share stories of the craziness and mishaps of the past few weeks. It seemed like everyone was in a good mood. Discussions of clients turned to football scores and digressed to observations about Mark's latest girlfriend. When the group ordered the third round, Lauren called it quits. "I'm good," she said. As the words came out of her mouth, she realized she believed them — literally, figuratively, and everywhere in between. She was good — good at her job, a good person, and happy with herself. Her heart and head were at peace. It was a nice place to be.

Her journal note that night:

First off, Suzie. I'm noticing how some friends come into my life for a time, but aren't meant to stay. She means well, but she's toxic. I just did a quick Internet search on toxic friendships. Here are my answers to the questions, with Suzie in mind.

Toxic Relationships
- Do your friends energize you, or drain your energy? *drain*
- Is your friend overly critical? *yes*
- Would you describe your friend as cynical and negative? *yes*
- Does your friend mostly complain or does he/she exhibit gratitude? *complain*
- Does your relationship seem competitive? *No.*
- Does he/she seem to enjoy hearing about your setbacks in your career, relationships, or finances? *Yes!*
- Does your friend show genuine interest in you and your future success, or is your failure of more interest? *She seeks drama, failure I guess.*
- Would you describe your friend's mentality as scarcity (not enough to go around) or abundance (more than enough)? *Scarcity.*

It's sad to realize Suzie isn't a healthy person to maintain as a friend. If birds of a feather flock together, I don't want to be toxic and a negative impact on others.

I am starting to like myself. It feels good to know what I want and make room for all of the elements of my abundant life. My instincts know what to do. I promise to trust them and course-correct when I take a wrong turn.

Feeling good. Really good.

Reflection and Analysis Generate
Small Steps, BIG Gains

Some people come into your life for a season and some for a lifetime. Suzie is a well-intentioned friend who is simply stuck in an old story. Lauren can share her new insights and discoveries with Suzie. It takes courage to be bold enough to teach our friends our new stories. If they appreciate the new insights and understand our goals, it's possible to educate our friends. But some people don't care to rewrite old stories and gain new perspectives. It requires yet more courage to create a healthy distance from those who may be toxic. Eliminate, or minimize, time with people who drain and deplete you. Some people produce energy. Others take energy away. Which are you?

Create Your Own Five Degrees of Change

There are two kinds of people in this world: Scarcity and Abundance.

Scarcity people believe there is only enough to go around. They horde, protect and are possessive over friends, money, opportunities and time because they believe there's a limited supply.

Abundance people believe the cup runneth over. There's more than enough and treasures are best when shared. They are generous, thoughtful and service-oriented.

Which are you?

There are two kinds of people in this world: Scarcity and Abundance.

Look at the list of Toxic Relationships questions, and answer them for yourself. Then, think of your closest friends and colleagues and answer the questions for them.

Who you choose to spend time with is the most important choice you make in your personal life and career. Choose carefully.

1. If you're a scarcity person, what images, examples or experiences can you focus on to notice abundance? Air? Words? Types of living things? What comes to mind when you think of abundance?

2. If you're an abundance person, how can you make an even bigger impact on the universe? How can you multiply your energy to expand your influence?
3. With whom do you associate? Do they add, take or neutralize your energy?
4. Who do you need to add to your circle of friends?
5. If you're in a toxic relationship, consider whom you allow into your life. How can you eliminate or minimize your time with those people?
6. Do you like yourself? Why? Why not?
7. What small changes can you begin to make to trust your intuition and operate at your full potential?

Additional Resources

Carnegie, D. How To Win Friends and Influence People by Dale Carnegie. Simon and Schuster. 2009.

Cloud, H. and Townsend, J. Safe People: How to Find Relationships That Are Good for You and Avoid Those That Aren't. Zonderman. 1996

Collins, J. Good to Great: Why Some Companies Make the Leap... and Others Don't. Harper Business. 2001.

Take Control
of Yourself

"Your life is the sum result of all the choices you make,
both consciously and unconsciously. If you can control the process
of choosing, you can take control of all aspects of your life.
You can find the freedom that comes from being in charge of yourself.

—Robert F. Bennett
Former US Senator

It's tempting to get hung up on things outside of our control, like the economy. Lauren has become more aware of her ability to choose thoughts, beliefs and actions that will move her closer to her goals and allow her to be more aligned with her deepest values. We watch Lauren gain new insight when she discovers the difference between what she controls and what she does not.

◆ ◆ ◆

Over the weekend, Lauren thought about how her perspective was changing so quickly; she sometimes felt unable to keep pace with all the new information. She often had more than a mere glimmer of seeing the world in a new light, but she continued to self-regulate, edit her thoughts and flag herself with reminders and caution signs. Lauren was looking forward to her meeting with Andrea, but thought a change of pace to bring them out of Lauren's office space might be in order.

Andrea agreed with Lauren to change their meeting venue to Buckley's. Making as simple a decision as a new meeting venue made Lauren feel in control, positive, and moving in the right direction.

"So, what did you discover over the past couple of days?" Andrea's queried.

"One thing is clear. I've been giving others permission to direct my career. That revelation has been enormous. I know I need to take back my life. It has been challenging for me to try to change during these weeks, but I really have made an effort. I still feel as if I'm fighting against my natural tendency towards a defeatist attitude. Whenever I feel overwhelmed or stressed — which seems frequently — I feel the futility of it all. I want to change, but it feels fake. Will it always feel like work? Will it ever be natural?"

Will it ever be natural?

"Remember our conversation about beliefs?" Andrea reminded. "Consider this: whatever you believe to be true either is true, or the belief in it makes it true."

"You mean, just because I dream it, it's true?" Lauren challenged her coach. "Like I can believe there's a new Mercedes parked in my space downstairs?" Lauren was taking the concept to the ridiculous.

Whatever you believe to be true either is true, or the belief in it makes it true.

"Not quite. Like us all, some of your beliefs are both tricky and slippery. Limiting beliefs, as we have discussed, are often the very things in our way and we are not always aware of them. We have to be constantly on the watch for what beliefs hold us back."

Lauren thought the whole concept sounded hokey, like those infomercials at 2:00 a.m. "It still sounds like disregarding the truth just to think positively."

"Fair enough. Let's use an example. Remember the Ladder of Leverage? The ladder with the pool of "stuff" at the bottom? Give me a limiting belief you have about yourself or your situation," encouraged Andrea.

"I am never going to be a Venture Partner at this firm."

"Perfect example. With that belief, you never will be. If you focus on never being a Venture Partner — you won't be. If you think you can't, you can't. The opposite is also true. We get results wherever we focus. If you believe you'll be Venture Partner, your energy and daily focus will support you. There are no guarantees, but your focus will either support or block you."

Lauren and Andrea went back and forth debating beliefs. Lauren argued her thoughts had nothing to do with the current situation. She still kept seeing Richard and Peter as the *real* problems — the barriers to her success. She struggled with getting around them, but the task appeared insurmountable.

"Let's look at this another way." Andrea drew a large bull's eye with three concentric circles on the back of the paper placemat. On the outermost circle, she wrote, "Area of no control," Lauren strained forward to view Andrea's drawing as Andrea turned it around to show her.

Andrea waited with pen in hand. "What don't you have **any** control over?"

"The weather," Lauren offered.

"Yes, the weather . . ." Andrea wrote that down under the heading. "What else?"

"The economy, the healthcare system, natural disasters, aging, my mother-in-law ..."

"We'll get to her in a second. You're on a roll. There are so many things you don't control. We've got a solid list here." She drew an arrow to the next concentric circle inward and wrote, "Area of Influence."

"You influence your mother-in-law, yes?" she asked smiling. Now she was teasing Lauren.

"To some extent...but not so much since my husband, my ex, Robert...er...Bob, left."

"What else, and who else, do you influence?" the coach probed.

"My kids, my team, my clients, my schedule, my attitude, my focus—"

"These are all good but the last two belong in the center circle. We're not there yet. Other items in the Area of Influence included the company, senior leaders, committees, neighbors, and vendors. You influence those people in proximity, but have no consistently direct access to total strangers."

"Now for the fun part — your Area of Total Control." Andrea was excited as she drew the inner most circle and an arrow pointing to it. "There's **one** thing in there. What is it?"

There are lots of things about *you* that *you* control.

"Me?"

"Yes! You! Here's the good news. There are a lot of things about **you** that **you** control[6]. Like what?" Andrea was poised to capture Lauren's responses.

"My attitude, my focus, my choices, my fitness, my thoughts, my time, my goals and aspirations…." Lauren was in the zone. The clarity of control over all of these things triggered her excitement. "My mood, my education, the people I spend time with, the use of my talents, my leadership. Even my storytelling, like we've talked about."

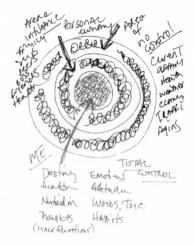

[6]Inspired by the Locus of Control theory in personality psychology referring to the extent to which individuals believe that they can control events that affect them. Originally developed by Julian B. Rotter in 1954.

Andrea swiftly filled the placemat with Lauren's responses, amazed by her awareness. "What does this represent for you, Lauren?"

Lauren looked hard at the pieces of her life all written on that one sheet of paper. "Wow! I spend the majority of my time worrying about things I can never control and neglect the things I can," she admitted. This was Lauren's *aha!* moment.

"Who has the power to change that?"

"I do."

| ***aha!* moment.**

Lauren felt as if a major burden had been lifted. *I choose to be the engineer of my life. I choose, and my choices determine my results.* As if afraid others might hear her secret, Lauren whispered across the table. "I often used to say, '**it is what it is,**' now I know, '**it is whatever I say it is.**' "

"That's enormous progress, Lauren."

"Suddenly, I'm feeling that all I have to do now is just get out of my own way!"

During her drive home, Lauren recorded her thoughts on a voice memo.

"Today was astonishing! I learned so many things. I'm taking control of my life and making big changes for the better through small, five degree modifications. Now I know what areas of my life are under my control, and have a good feeling about what the future holds. I *can* choose, so I **do** choose."

| **It is whatever I say it is.**

Reflection and Analysis Generate Small Steps, BIG Gains

Most of us have plenty of work to do in the Area of Control. Let's not judge others on how well they are managing their lives. Rather, focus on the five degree shifts we can make within and commit to making progress ourselves. The combination of tools and visuals is helping Lauren to fully grasp the concept of self-control and regulation so she can effectively make the small shifts for big sustainable gains.

Create Your Own Five Degrees of Change

Record your answers to these questions:

1. What have you been focused on that you do not control?
2. Which circle consumes most of your energy?
3. Many people who are frustrated in life put the majority of their energy in the outer circle and virtually none in the center. Why relinquish the only control we truly have? How can you relate?
4. What elements in your "center circle" (what you control about you) will you make progress on this week? (Pick one or two)

Area of Influence
- Work
- Direct Reports
- Coworkers
- Boss
- Committees
- Peers
- Senior Mgt.
- Customers
- Teams
- Service Projects
- Health
- Family
- Friends
- Neighbors

Area of Control

YOU

Area of Total Control
- Thoughts
- Beliefs
- Choices
- Attitude
- Meaning making
- Priorities
- Work/Life
- Preparation
- Daily habits
- Goals
- Questions you ask
- Physical health
- Your network
- Role as a leader
- Ownership of self
- Commitments
- Knowledge
- Contribution
- Leverage Strengths

Area of NO Control

Traffic	Market	Death/Aging
Weather	Strangers	Competition
Economy	Natural Disaster	Accidents

Additional Resources

Tichy, N. and Sherman, S. Control Your Destiny or Someone Else Will (Collins Business Essentials). Harper Business. 2005.

Robbins, A. Awaken the Giant Within: How to Take Immediate Control of Your Mental, Emotional, Physical and Financial Destiny! Free Press. 1992.

Duhigg, C. The Power of Habit: Why We Do What We Do in Life and Business. Random House. 2012.

Share Your Brilliance

"When you know better, you do better."

—Maya Angelou

American Poet

Once you realize you have control and the power to be a force for good and a light in the world you have a choice to make. You either step up and be a part of the solution or sit back and remain a part of the problem. "Understanding" you have power and can create change is the booby prize. Taking action and finding ways to add value beyond measure is what matters.

❖ ❖ ❖

Still groggy, Lauren forced herself to roll over and sit up. Her eyes focused on the running shoes and socks she had laid out the night before. "I choose." She put on her shoes and walked stiffly downstairs to the treadmill, moving quietly, not wanting to wake the kids.

She smiled at the bright yellow split-arrow turn sign Danny put up on the basement door that said, "Five Degree Turn," switched on the TV, set the volume at a whisper, and started the treadmill. The slow walk became a jog, then a run. But as fast as she ran, her mind ran faster. Random thoughts came and went as she thought through

"Understanding" is the booby prize.

all of the things she felt were holding her back: the craziness at the office, her entire career, staff, clients, and email. *Why was her schedule packed so tightly? Did she need to work such late nights? And what about the daily caffeine overload?* She broke into a fast sprint. *How can I better manage Richard?*

Andrea's voice continually entered her thoughts. She tried to

I choose.

rewrite her own questions. *What are the better questions?* Lauren stopped the treadmill abruptly and leaned over, resting her hands on her knees, feeling the sweat drip down her neck and listening to her heavy breathing. Write a new story? The voice echoed her breath. Write a new story. Write a new story! *"I'm at a*

Write a new story.

crossroads. My question is: What am I willing to do to have the life I want? How must I author my new story? What kind of story will it be?" She smiled at the endless possibilities of triumph, power and joy her stories could tell.

◆ ◆ ◆

Lauren got to work with enough time to thoughtfully greet James, fire up her laptop, and grab a green tea from the break room. Her head was whirling with innovative solutions and plans. She opened up a new PowerPoint presentation and began creating visuals and models of her ideas. She interrupted her brainstorm, walked down the hall and took her seat at the conference room table ten minutes early. The rest of the team straggled in around 9:30. Finally at 9:45, showing no concern and without apology, Richard sauntered in. Of course Lauren noticed his tardiness, but chose not to dwell on it. She took a deep, cleansing breath to release her shoulder tension. *I control me, not someone outside myself,* she thought, pulling the cap off her favorite fountain pen.

With a broad sweep of his hand Richard announced, "Peter is going to run the meeting today. I'm pleased to be handing the reins over to him. He is by far our strongest leader, besides me, of course." Making sure his predictable attempts at humor were met appropriately, Richard, looked around at his team. They forced a laugh and quickly lowered their eyes to their blank legal pads.

"Hey, team, we're going to rock and roll, right on!" Peter's awkwardness was transmitted to everyone present, making all uncomfortable. For a moment, Lauren empathized with the new Venture Partner. At the same time, it dawned on her that his rather glaring lack of experience and ineloquent full display of it for Richard and the team could be his undoing. What did that mean for her, or, how could she parlay it into a better outcome for herself?

Though on their best behavior, this particular meeting was painful for all. When Peter asked for questions, no one dared say anything to prolong the obvious agony. It was pretty clear that wrapping it up quickly was in everyone's best interests. Peter's first meeting was perhaps the quietest on record.

"Allrighty, then. We're all on the same page and ready to roll." Peter made his way towards the conference room door and put up his right hand to encourage high fives, nodding and winking to each of the staff as they left the room. "You're the best." Jack stood directly in front of Lauren as they exited, rolling his eyes. It was all she could do to resist an exchange of sarcastic comments. As she went through the door she responded with the requisite high five. Out of the corner of her eye on her way to her office, she noticed Richard and Peter complete their high five with a mutual shoulder slap. "Great job, Pete," gushed Richard. "You really

Her focus was on creating a new path.

set the tone for the future here." Lauren found their interaction momentarily irritating, but was no longer resentful. Her focus was on creating a new path. The positive anticipation she had about presenting her ideas to Richard – strategies and innovative ways to add more value – consumed her.

◆ ◆ ◆

auren was immaturely encouraged that others in the meeting were also clearly not thrilled with Peter's performance. Nevertheless, it didn't matter anymore whether she liked him or felt that he could do his job well. Her sights were set on the future and how she could contribute. She got back to her desk, answered a few emails, and sent an email to Richard requesting a meeting to discuss her future at DEG.

The next morning, she met Richard in his office. She'd spent the last night rehearsing the conversation in her head, and reviewed it during her commute. She knew what she wanted — what she **needed** to be successful.

"So, kiddo, what brings you into my office so bright and early?" Richard began.

"Well, first, I wanted to thank you for the great coaching support." The pumping adrenaline made Lauren a bit shaky. "It has opened my eyes and been extremely helpful."

"Super. Glad it worked out. Thanks for stopping by and letting me know, Els." It was clear from his tone that he wanted to cut the meeting short. Lauren was determined to make her case and handed him a first-class presentation.

"Actually, Richard, there's more. Lots more. I've been giving a lot of thought to my career path and how I can contribute even more to DEG. I want to propose some changes I think would benefit us both." Richard was intrigued; the only proposals Lauren brought him were well-developed, clear winners. "Go on."

"You know that I have tremendous experience in the healthcare IT sector and maintain close contacts with several influencers of Market Leaders. I think DEG should leverage this currently untapped, fast-growing sector. Long-term demographic trends make this market particularly attractive for private equity investments, and I'm the right person to head up this new division for DEG."

"Wow. That's — quite an idea," said Richard's slowly as he leafed through the material and thought through the concept. "Is this all about becoming Venture Partner?"

"Yes — and no. Here's what I propose: You and I set benchmarks and goals for the new division for the next six months. You let me take four of my current team members with me, and **when** the goals are achieved, we discuss a new title that, while not necessarily Venture Partner, equitably reflects my contributions to the firm. I want to develop a new kind of career path — one that allows me to offer my strengths and skills."

> **I want to develop a new kind of career path—one that allows me to offer my strengths and skills.**

Richard laughed warmly. "It sounds good, Els. I'm all for anything that benefits the firm and keeps you happy. Send me a comprehensive proposal by the end of the week. If it adds up on paper, we can move forward the first of next month."

"Great. I'll make sure you get what you need. This is going to be a huge win for everyone," Lauren added confidently.

She stood up to leave. Then a question crossed her mind. "May I ask you something, Richard? It has me stumped and I just can't figure —"

"Shoot."

"Why do you call me 'Els?'"

Richard laughed. "You really don't know? Your middle name is Louise. Lauren Louise. Two 'L's.' Els. Get it?"

"*That's* it? I never thought of that!" Lauren was clearly amused, and grinned broadly.

"You got it!"

"Thanks for telling me. I've wondered for years."

Lauren beamed as she left Richard's office. *I'm back!* She couldn't wait to share her success with Andrea at their coaching session. As soon as Andrea walked into Lauren's office and shut the door, Lauren raised her hands in the air like a marathon winner, positively bursting with pride. "I'm in control!"

> **I choose.**

Andrea laughed, thrilled to see Lauren enthusiastic and positive. "Fantastic, Lauren! Tell me what's been going on!"

"I get it. I totally understand — **I choose**. I choose my beliefs, my stories, and my-my —"searching for the right word "—**future!**"

"Wow! What caused this breakthrough?"

"The bull's-eye image. The storytelling. The beliefs. It makes perfect sense. I've been spending my days upset and resentful about things that will never change."

"What are you going to do?"

"I already did it! I stayed up last night working on ideas, got up early this morning, put them on paper, talked with Richard, and told him I wanted to head a new healthcare IT division — it's a win-win for me and the firm," she answered.

"That's great Lauren! Are you ready for this new challenge?"

"Totally. I've been thinking about doing something like this for a long time, and didn't think it would be possible here at DEG. But then I questioned those notions, and decided to approach Richard. This new plan allows me to stay with the firm I've invested six years in, **and** I get to start a division in an area I'm passionate about." Lauren was abuzz with positive energy as she thought about what was yet to come.

"You've made wonderful progress," Andrea beamed. "I don't think we really need to schedule another appointment. How about we reconnect if something comes up or you feel you need to."

"I agree. I'm feeling confident about where things are right now," Lauren confirmed. "I'll keep you posted and call if I need help in the future, but I think I'm ready to take it from here."

Lauren stood up to give trusted Coach Lombardi a warm hug. She didn't really want her to leave.

◆◆◆

Reflection and Analysis Generate Small Steps, BIG Gains

Lauren's new-found confidence enabled her career growth. She took full responsibility for her career and purpose at work. This framework enables her to bravely articulate new ideas or innovative solutions to problems. Heretofore, Lauren's performance was inhibited by her own self-sabotage, judgment, and focus on things that won't help her. She is waking up to realize the only way to stand out and make an impact is to use her gifts and refocus on what really matters. Her disappointment resulted from overindulgence on self and minimal focus on purpose. Lauren's freedom and power are now generated from her new belief: I make a difference. I matter. However doubtful and apprehensive, Lauren was ready. She took the five degree steps needed to make necessary changes. Now it's time to continue practicing on her own.

> **Disappointment resulted from overindulgence on self and minimal focus on purpose.**

Create Your Own Five Degrees of Change

From what to wear in the morning, to major, life-changing decisions, we all make hundreds of choices each day. When it seems impossible to choose between alternatives, approach the process methodically. You can even use a decision-making metric like the one suggested here. Find a process that works for you!

> **We all make hundreds of choices each day.**

1. **Take one five-degree step at a time.** Stay focused on what you want to complete, and *do* something. *Pick up the phone. Put on your running shoes. Start writing the draft.* One step at a time.

2. **Explore all choices.** There are plenty of choices. If there aren't any, create some! Don't discount any options in the initial stages of your decision-making process. Having only one choice is not a choice. Two choices present a dilemma: this or that. Brainstorm three or more choices, weigh each one, and commit to one.

3. **Listen to your gut.** Your intuition is rarely wrong. What was your first thought? Take in information intellectually; make decisions intuitively. Trust yourself.

4. **Let it rest.** Once you make a decision, put it away for a day or two and then revisit it. Does it still feel right? If

so, commit fully to the choice you made. If not, explore further to find a better solution.

5. **Take action.** Feeling confident in the process and your decision, you should now move boldly to making it a reality. Schedule it and make it happen. Move!

Record your answers to these questions:

- *What is your goal? What's the lingering idea you've had for a while that you really want to go after?*
- *What are you willing to do to have the life you want?*
- *How can you make your vision a win-win for you and your company?*
- *What creative solutions exist?*
- *Brainstorm the possibilities. Never settle. Know there is always a way.*

Additional Resources

Heath, C. and D. Switch: How to Change Things When Change Is Hard. Crown Business. 2010.

Lee, B. Savvy: Thirty Days to a Different Perspective. Alliance Press. 1992.

Demonstrate Emotional Intelligence

"But once you are in that field, emotional intelligence emerges as a much stronger predictor of who will be most successful, because it is how we handle ourselves in our relationships that determines how well we do once we are in a given job."

—Daniel Goleman
Psychologist, Best Selling Author

When someone makes positive changes in life — even five degrees at a time — people notice. Lauren's improvements make a lot of people notice.

◆ ◆ ◆

Richard was among the first to see the "new Els." Lauren strode forward with apparent new energy and purpose, single-handedly starting a new Healthcare Investment division, which took root within weeks. She was able to purposefully meet this interim goal and turn a profit well before the six-month period she targeted. She regularly joined the lunchtime running group and expressed a positive team attitude.

While Lauren didn't wish "Peter Principle" to fail, nevertheless, he fumbled in his Venture Partner role. He could see it coming, and gave notice to DEG – leaving to 'pursue other interests.'

On the home front, she had dinner with the kids most nights, they played and shared lots of quality time. It took little time for Lauren to catch up on her mortgage payments, and begin building back her retirement savings.

"Let's go to the bookstore," Lauren suggested to the kids one Saturday. "There's a book I want to pick up called **Take Time for Your Life**, by Cheryl Richardson."

"Sure, Mom." They liked the mall and agreed readily.

"Stay together in the Fiction/Mystery/Fantasy/Sci-Fi section," Lauren whispered to the kids. Grinning, they quickly walked towards the back of the bookstore.

After Lauren found the book she sought, she browsed the tables. Her eye caught the "New Fiction" sign. It had been years since she indulged in a great novel, and suddenly she felt like checking out the latest titles. As she thumbed through a brand new page-turner, she heard a familiar voice and looked up.

"Andrea!" she exclaimed as she gave her coach a big hug.

"Hey, Lauren, it's so great to see you! How are you?"

"Oh, Andrea, so much has changed since we spoke last. I got the new healthcare division started; it has several clients in the post-closing phase. The division is creating a positive stir in the firm. I'm a lot more hands-on with clients — which I love. And best of all, I feel like I'm really contributing and appreciated. I've been working out regularly and building back my savings."

> **Making a meaningful contribution is worth more than any title.**

"I'm so happy for you." From what she described, Lauren's personal and professional transformation was significant, despite the short time since the two had become acquainted, and Andrea was delighted to see it. "Are you still working with Richard?"

"Of course," she smiled. "But his antics don't get to me anymore. I'm doing what I love with a team of fantastic, capable people. I'm really centered. I'm still not Venture Partner, but truly enjoying my work. Making a meaningful contribution is worth more than any title."

"That's wonderful!"

"I don't know how to thank you, Andrea. You sparked the beginning of the best phase of my life. I'm not sure I'd be where I am now without your help. Learning from you all the useful concepts and practical tools I can use to change my story, attitude, and my life. And the art of practicing the five degree principle! You've been incredibly helpful!"

"Perhaps I opened new doorways of thinking for you, Lauren, but you walked through them. It was *you* who wrote the new story for yourself, and you didn't let anyone hold you back. I'm delighted to see how you've taken charge of your life."

Lauren's phone rang. "I'm sorry...it's Richard...I have to take it."

"Els! So glad I caught you. I wanted to call before the end of the day. I just got out of a Partners' meeting. All the Partners have been watching your progress with the new healthcare division and really like the direction it's taking for the firm. Your innovation and leadership are impressive. We all agree: you'd be a valuable Venture Partner. What do you say?"

Reflection and Analysis Generate
Small Steps, BIG Gains

Every step or decision we make in life adds up. If we take the time to closely examine the steps and missteps, decisions, and choices, good or bad, we can improve upon our innate Emotional Intelligence (EI), further develop it, and score a higher quotient. Each incremental improvement in our EI helps us further down the road improve our decision-making and discernment about making choices best for ourselves.

> **Every step or decision we make in life adds up.**

Daniel Goleman[7] introduced the EI model, which focuses on a wide array of competencies and skills that drive leadership performance. Goleman's four main self- and other- constructs can help provide direction and discipline to guide you through life's constant array of decision trees.

1. Self-awareness – the ability to read one's emotions and recognize their impact while using gut feelings to guide decisions.
2. Self-management – involves controlling one's emotions and impulses and adapting to changing circumstances.
3. Social awareness – the ability to sense, understand, and react to others' emotions while comprehending social networks.
4. Relationship management – the ability to inspire, influence, and develop others while managing conflict.

Create Your Own Five Degrees of Change

Record your responses to these questions

Which Emotional Intelligence (EI) muscles do *you* need to build? Self-awareness? Self-management? Social awareness? Relationship management?

Answer true or false to these questions to ask yourself if you demonstrate emotional intelligence[8]:

1. In my group of friends, I often don't notice the dynamics of the social circle.
2. When I am upset, I struggle to pinpoint exactly what's bothering me.
3. There are lots of things I would like to change about myself. Generally, I'm not satisfied with myself.

---

[7]Goleman, D. Working With Emotional Intelligence. New York: Bantam Books 1998
[8]Adapted from Psychology.about.com *What's your EQ?*

4. When I make mistakes, I often criticize my abilities and myself.
5. I feel uncomfortable in emotionally charged situations.
6. I tend to avoid confrontations. When I am involved in a confrontation, I become extremely anxious.
7. I am generally aloof and detached until I really get to know a person.
8. I tend to overreact to minor problems.
9. I feel insecure about my own skills, talents, and abilities.
10. I would not describe myself as a good judge of character.
11. When making an important decision, I tend to rely on direction from other people.
12. My co-worker has a habit that annoys me. Instead of talking with my co-worker directly I suffer in silence and hope it goes away.
13. I've been feeling stressed out at work and haven't finished projects as quickly as I should. I'm angry that my boss hasn't noticed how overworked I am.
14. When I'm upset, everyone knows it. I need to work on my poker face.

More "false" responses means higher emotional intelligence. People with emotional intelligence tend to be good at interpreting, understanding, and acting upon emotions. They are usually quite good at dealing with social or emotional conflicts, expressing their feelings, and dealing with emotional situations.

It's important to remember that no matter how you answered these questions, there is always room to improve your emotional intelligence (EI). Consider areas where you are not as strong and find ways to improve. Build the EI muscles with intentional practice. Notice how you feel, discover *why* and create choices of how you want to respond. Refocus on your goal and choose the option that best helps you achieve it. Take stock of your strengths and find ways to continue to build and develop your EI further.

Refocus on your goal and choose the option that best helps you achieve it.

EPILOGUE

Small shifts.

Say this – silence that.

Sit at the meeting table – not the periphery conference room chairs.

Be social – demonstrate camaraderie. Stay sober. Be professional.

Eat this – avoid that. Your health is the foundation of your strength. Feed yourself fuel to sustain the energy to do your work.

Respond to this – laugh off that. Don't take yourself too seriously: "Blessed are those who can laugh at themselves, for they shall never cease to be amused." (Anonymous)

"Blessed are those who can laugh at themselves, for they shall never cease to be amused." (Anonymous).

Act on this – pause on that. Think before you act. Professional maturity lies in the gap between cause and effect.

Listen deeply – not just to what's happening on the surface. Listen to the choice of words, the tone of voice, the nonverbal gestures and hear the soul of the message.

Focus on purpose – not pride. Service – not self. Only after our goals expand outward, beyond self-interest, to the greater good, do we experience a real sense of worth.

"Humility is not thinking less of ourselves, it is thinking of ourselves less."

Be humble – not arrogant. As British scholar and author C.S. Lewis says, "Humility is not thinking less of ourselves, it is thinking of ourselves less."

Lauren is flourishing. On her personal, home, and career fronts, she's showing signs of mastery in the art of making small, perceptual shifts. This skill is evidenced quite well by her successes and the notice they're garnering in her workplace. Her power was trampled on by some unexpected (but fairly predictable) life/work twists and turns, but it's flowing back, and she is buoyed by her accomplishments. She's picking up the valuable momentum she'll need for the inevitable bumps and turns in the road ahead. The tide is turning for Lauren. Her energy and fervor are returning, she's on a roll, gaining traction, and scoring points to help the Lauren team win the game.

With Andrea's help, Lauren has learned to rid herself of the weight of toxic, unhealthy self-talk and relationships, and has learned to identify when her thoughts begin moving in a negative direction. A quick five-degree turn may be all she needs to steer those thoughts in the right direction. She's become more open-minded, revealing to herself a bigger, clearer, brighter picture. She's listening more deeply and asking more of the right questions. Lauren has climbed so many rungs up and out of her stuff at the bottom of her personal ladder of leverage, those limiting beliefs have begun to palpably dissipate. Her shift of focus allowed room for creativity and inventiveness that long lay dormant. Her pro-active design and implementation of the successful Healthcare Division proves this point.

Lauren knew she needed to embrace new possibilities, but didn't have the tools. The ideas in Andrea's all-important Coaching Binder have given Lauren the impetus she needed. To Do, To Don't, To Delegate; the Formula for Fulfillment; and the Roads of Resentment and Resolution illustration (which will remain affixed to

Anything is possible.

her refrigerator door for the kids to benefit from as well) will serve Lauren in becoming a positive agent of personal change and getting back on track when the going gets rough. These tools have helped her meet her vital, deserved, and specifically-stated goal of becoming Venture Partner. While Lauren worked hard to get there, the promotion to Venture Partner didn't occur because she was so focused on it that it would inevitably elude her. No one wrote this new story for Lauren but Lauren herself. Her happier, healthier outlook and activities have returned her sparkle. Even her children see how she's embracing hobbies she once had shelved. It feels as though there might even be room for her to embrace a new relationship. At the moment, Lauren feels anything is possible!

The unexpected happens to us all, we all experience setbacks – it's just part of the human condition. What's different now is that Lauren is armed with new tools to help her refocus her lens, reassess old stories and write new ones, establish and stick to priorities, and regain balance and control. Lauren has done the work, but all of it has largely been a matter of Coach Lombardi encouraging her to make the right five degree changes in attitude, perceptions and strategic action to achieve measurable and desired outcomes.

Make the right five degree changes in attitude, perceptions and strategic action to achieve measurable and desired outcomes.

Lauren has developed better emotional intelligence, and the courage and knowledge that she can continue to make positive changes. Ironically or not, it was a collection of small, five degree turns of Lauren's inner compass that resulted in her quantum leap forward.

❖ ❖ ❖

CITATIONS
AND
ACKNOWLEDGMENTS

Chapter One:

"In order to succeed, people need a sense of self-efficacy, to struggle together with resilience to meet the inevitable obstacles and inequities of life."

—Albert Bandura, Psychologist and Teacher

Albert Bandura is a psychologist, the David Starr Jordan Professor Emeritus of Social Science in Psychology at Stanford University. Over almost six decades, he has been responsible for contributions to many fields of psychology, including social cognitive theory, therapy and personality psychology, and was also influential in the transition between behaviorism and cognitive psychology. He is known as the originator of social learning theory and the theory of self-efficacy, and is also responsible for the influential 1961 Bobo doll experiment. A 2002 survey ranked Bandura as the fourth most-frequently cited psychologist of all time, behind B. F. Skinner, Sigmund Freud, and Jean Piaget, and as the most cited living one. Bandura is widely described as the greatest living psychologist, and as one of the most influential psychologists of all time. In 2008 Bandura won the Grawemeyer Award in psychology.

Chapter Two:

"If the career you have chosen has some unexpected inconvenience, console yourself by reflecting that no career is without them."
—Jane Fonda, American Actress and Fitness Buff

Jane Fonda is an American actress, writer, political activist, former fashion model, and fitness guru. She rose to fame in the 1960s with films such as Barbarella and Cat Ballou. She has won two Academy Awards and received several other movie awards and nominations during more than 50 years as an actress. She also produced and starred in over 20 exercise videos released between 1982 and 1995, and once again in 2010. She describes herself as a liberal and a feminist. In 2005, Fonda worked alongside Robin Morgan and Gloria Steinem to co-found the Women's Media Center, an organization that works to amplify the voices of women in the media through advocacy, media and leadership training, and the creation of original content. Fonda currently serves on the board of the organization.

Chapter Three:

"You gain strength, courage and confidence by every experience in which you really stop to look fear in the face…You must do the thing you cannot do."
—Eleanor Roosevelt, First Lady and Civil Rights Advocate

Anna Eleanor Roosevelt was the First Lady of the United States from 1933 to 1945. She supported the New Deal policies of her husband, and became an advocate for civil rights. After her husband's death in 1945, Roosevelt continued to be an international author, speaker, politician, and activist for the New Deal coalition. She was a delegate to the UN General Assembly from 1945 to 1952.

Chapter Four:

"The key is not to prioritize what's on your schedule but to schedule your priorities."

—Stephen R. Covey, Leadership Authority and Best Selling Author

Recognized as one of Time magazine's 25 most influential Americans, Stephen R. Covey has dedicated his life to demonstrating how every person can truly control their destiny with profound, yet straightforward guidance. As an internationally respected leadership authority, family expert, teacher, organizational consultant, and author, his advice has given insight to millions. Stephen Covey is the author of the best-selling books, The Seven Habits of Highly Effective People, First Things First, Principle-Centered Leadership, and The Seven Habits of Highly Effective Families. In 2004, Covey released The 8th Habit. Stephen Covey sadly passed on July 16, 2012.

Chapter Five:

"Each of us, every waking hour, is called upon to say no, whether to friends or family members, to our bosses, employees, or co-workers, or to ourselves. Whether and how we say no determines the very quality of our lives. It is perhaps the most important word to learn to say gracefully and effectively."

—William Ury, Mediator, Writer and Negotiation Expert

Over the last 30 years, Bill Ury has served as a negotiation adviser and mediator in conflicts ranging from corporate mergers to wildcat strikes in a Kentucky coal mine to ethnic wars in the Middle East, the Balkans, and the former Soviet Union. With former president Jimmy Carter, he co-founded the International Negotiation Network, a non-governmental body seeking to end civil wars around the world. William L. Ury co-founded Harvard's Program on Negotiation and is currently a Senior Fellow of the Harvard Negotiation Project. He is the author of The Power of a Positive No: How to Say No & Still Get to Yes (2007) and co-author (with Roger Fisher) of Getting to Yes: Negotiating Agreement Without Giving In, an eight-million-copy bestseller translated into over thirty languages.

Chapter Six:

"What I am looking for is not out there, it is in me."

—Helen Keller, American Author and Lecturer

Helen Adams Keller was an American author, political activist, and lecturer. She was the first deaf/blind person to earn a Bachelor of Arts degree. A prolific author, Keller was well traveled, and was outspoken in her anti-war convictions. A member of the Socialist Party of America and the Industrial Workers of the World, she campaigned for women's suffrage, labor rights, socialism, and other radical left causes. She was inducted into the Alabama Women's Hall of Fame in 1971.

Chapter Seven:

"Action expresses priorities."

—Mahatma Gandhi, Leader of the Indian Nationalist Movement

Mohandas Karamchand Gandhi, commonly known as Mahatma Gandhi, was the pre-eminent leader of Indian nationalism in British-ruled India. Employing non-violent civil disobedience, Gandhi led India to independence and inspired movements for non-violence, civil rights and freedom across the world. A lifelong opponent of "communalism" (i.e. basing politics on religion) he reached out widely to all religious groups. Assuming leadership of the Indian National Congress in 1921, Gandhi led nationwide campaigns for easing poverty, expanding women's rights, building religious and ethnic amity, ending untouchability, increasing economic self-reliance, and above all for achieving Swaraj—the independence of India from British domination.

Chapter Eight:

"Perhaps if one really knew when one was happy one would know the things that were necessary for one's life."

—Joanna Field, Author, A Life of One's Own

Marion Milner was a British author and psychoanalyst. Outside psychotherapeutic circles, she is better known by her pseudonym, Joanna Field, as a pioneer of introspective journaling. She studied at University College, London where she graduated with a 1st Class degree in psychology in 1924. In 1926, Milner began an introspective journal that later became one of her best-known books, A Life of One's Own (eventually published under the name Joanna Field in 1934).

Chapter Nine:

"We thought that we had the answers, it was the questions we had wrong."

—Bono, Musician and Humanitarian

Paul David Hewson, most commonly known by his stage name Bono, is an Irish singer, musician, and humanitarian best known for being the main vocalist of the Dublin-based rock band U2. Outside the band, he has collaborated and recorded with numerous artists, is managing director and a managing partner of Elevation Partners, and has refurbished and owns The Clarence Hotel in Dublin with The Edge. Bono is also widely known for his activism concerning Africa, for which he co-founded DATA, EDUN, the ONE Campaign and Product Red. He has organized and played in several benefit concerts and has met with influential politicians. He has been nominated for the Nobel Peace Prize, was granted an honorary knighthood by Queen Elizabeth II of the United Kingdom, and was named as a Person of the Year by Time, among other awards and nominations.

Chapter Ten:

"The happiness of your life depends on the quality of your thoughts."

—Marcus Aurelius Antoninus, Roman Emperor
and Philosopher

Marcus Aurelius was Roman Emperor from 161 to 180 AD. He ruled with Lucius Verus as co-emperor from 161 until Verus' death in 169. He was the last of the "Five Good Emperors", and is also considered one of the most important Stoic philosophers. Marcus Aurelius' Stoic tome Meditations, written in Greek while on campaign between 170 and 180, is still revered as a literary monument to a philosophy of service and duty, describing how to find and preserve equanimity in the midst of conflict by following nature as a source of guidance and inspiration.

Chapter Eleven:

"We are the stories we tell ourselves."

—Shekhar Kapur, Filmmaker

Shekhar Kapur is a critically acclaimed Indian film director and producer. He rose to popularity with the Hindi language movie Bandit Queen based upon the life of Phoolan Devi, an infamous Indian outlaw. His historical biopics of Queen Elizabeth (Elizabeth and its sequel The Golden Age) garnered 7 Academy Award nominations, including Best Picture and Best Actress for Cate Blanchett.

Chapter Twelve:

"Don't be trapped by dogma – which is living with the results of other people's thinking. Don't let the noise of other's opinions drown out your own inner voice. And most important, have the courage to follow your heart and intuition."

—Steve Jobs, American Entrepreneur and
Apple Computer Co-Founder

Steven Paul "Steve" Jobs was an American businessman, designer and inventor. He is best known as the co-founder, chairman, and chief executive officer of Apple Inc. Through Apple, he was widely recognized as a charismatic pioneer of the personal computer revolution and for his influential career in the computer and consumer electronics fields. Jobs also co-founded and served as chief executive of Pixar Animation Studios.

Chapter Thirteen:

"Your life is the sum result of all the choices you make, both consciously and unconsciously. If you can control the process of choosing, you can take control of all aspects of your life. You can find the freedom that comes from being in charge of yourself."

—Robert F. Bennett, Former US Senator

Robert Foster "Bob" Bennett is a lobbyist, a former United States Senator from Utah, and a member of the Republican Party. Bennett held chairmanships and senior positions on a number of key Senate committees, including the Banking, Housing and Urban Affairs Committee, Appropriations Committee, Rules and Administration Committee, Energy and Natural Resources Committee, and Joint Economic Committee.

Chapter Fourteen:

"When you know better, you do better."

—Maya Angelou, American Poet

Dr. Maya Angelou, born Marguerite Ann Johnson, is an American author and poet. She has published six autobiographies, five books of essays, numerous books of poetry, and is credited with a long list of plays, movies, and television shows. She is one of the most decorated writers of her generation, with dozens of awards and over thirty honorary doctoral degrees. Angelou is best known for her series of autobiographies, which focus on her childhood and early adult experiences. The first and most highly acclaimed, I Know Why the Caged Bird Sings (1969), tells of her first seventeen years, and brought her international recognition and acclaim. Since 1991, she has taught at Wake Forest University in Winston-Salem, North Carolina, where she holds the first lifetime Reynolds Professorship of American Studies.

Chapter Fifteen:

"But once you are in that field, emotional intelligence emerges as a much stronger predictor of who will be most successful, because it is how we handle ourselves in our relationships that determines how well we do once we are in a given job."

—Daniel Goleman, Psychologist, Best Selling Author

Daniel Jay Goleman is an author, psychologist, and science journalist. For twelve years, he wrote for The New York Times, specializing in psychology and brain sciences. He is the author of more than 10 books on psychology, education, science, and leadership. Goleman authored the internationally best-selling book, Emotional Intelligence (1995, Bantam Books), which spent more than one-and-a-half years on the New York Times Best Seller list. Goleman developed the argument that non-cognitive skills can matter as much as I.Q. for workplace success in "Working with Emotional Intelligence" (1998, Bantam Books), and for leadership effectiveness in "Primal Leadership" (2001, Harvard Business School Press).

ABOUT THE AUTHOR

Founder and CEO of **bridge between, inc.** — a specialized executive coaching firm focused on behavioral change and leadership effectiveness — Shannon Cassidy helps leaders bridge the gap from where they are now to where they want to be. Ms. Cassidy works with clients to develop strength-based action plans for leading high-performance teams, navigating corporate politics, communicating with vision and inspiration, and creating win-win conflict resolutions.

Before establishing **bridge between, inc.**, Ms. Cassidy spent several years as a corporate leader. Having received rave reviews from audiences and meeting planners for such speeches as **Quality Questions, The Story of Success**, and **Power of One**, Shannon has become a much-sought-after keynote speaker at national conferences, women's events, and corporate retreats. A Turner Broadcasting executive said, *"Shannon is a secret weapon to any company looking to build best in class teams and high performers."*

Shannon earned her Business and Professional Communication degree at the University of Rhode Island and received her certification as an Executive Corporate Coach through CCUI, accredited by the International Coach Federation. After participating in Harvard Law School's Corporate Negotiation Training Program (PON), Shannon earned her Corporate Negotiation Training certificate. She is a member of the National Speakers Association (NSA), the National Association of Multi-Ethnicity in Communications (NAMIC), and Women in Cable and Telecommunications (WICT), where her mentoring programs earned the reputation of being highly effective and successful. She has penned several articles and is co-author of **Discover Your Inner Strength**. Forbes.com featured Shannon as one of the Top Five Coaches in Philadelphia, where she makes her home with her husband and two children and is an active community volunteer.

SERVICES OFFERED:
Executive Coaching
Keynote Speaking
Meeting Facilitation (retreats, offsites, mentoring programs)
Training delivery

CONTACT INFORMATION:
bridge between, inc.
Connecting potential to performance
Two Penn Center | Suite 200 | Philadelphia, PA | 19102 |
Website: www.bridgebetween.com
Facebook: www.facebook.com/bridgebetweeninc
Phone Number: 610-431-2888
For information please contact: service@bridgebetween.com

◆ ◆ ◆